# LOUIS NO. 1

## The Life and Legend of Louis St. Germaine

by

## Tom Hollatz

970.3
Ho

*LARANMARK PRESS*

A division of Laranmark, Inc          Neshkoro, Wisconsin

*LARANMARK PRESS*

A division of
Laranmark, Inc.
211 Main Street
Box 253
Neshkoro, Wisconsin 54960

Copyright © 1984 by Tom Hollatz
ISBN: 0-910937-17-6 (Hardcover)
ISBN: 0-910937-18-4 (Softcover)

First Printing May 1984

Printed by
Worzalla Publishing
3535 Jefferson
Stevens Point, Wisconsin

# Table of Contents

# Acknowledgements

A very special thanks goes to several people who contributed to *Louis No. 1* including the family of Louis St. Germaine: daughters Flossie Allen and Margaret Lilly; and sons William and Richard St. Germaine.

Also thanks to Tom Newcomb, Maylin and Kathy Ruff, Les Rusch, Harold "Tuffy" Titus, Arthur "Bud" Knudtson, Jerry Loar, Dennis Robertson, Mrs. Peg Dillman, Howard "Pop" Dean, Jim Peck, Harvey Bagley, Bill Gleason, Ted Williams, Albert Cobe, Mabel Gauthier, Ben Guthrie, Franklin Cisney, Mike Aschenbrener, Hiram Valliere, Agnes Valliere, Joyce Laabs, and the Durkee "Spice King" Jim Ford.

# LOUIS NO. 1

## The Life and Legend of
## Louis St. Germaine:
## A Native American

*To his children*
*Flossie, Margie, Richard, and Billy*
*who walk tall and proud*

**Indian,** n. 1. Also called American Indian, Red Indian, a member of the aboriginal race of America or of any of the aboriginal North and South American stocks, usually excluding the Eskimos.

*—— The Random House*
*Dictionary of the English Language:*
*The Unabridged Edition*

*Chippewa Man*
*Spot-stiched leggings, floral shoulder bag and aprons, moccasins*
*and turban decorations.*

*Louis No. 1*

*Blessed is the man who has found his work.*

—— Thomas Carlyle

*Chippewa Beadwork*

*Thousands and millions of men exploit what is not really theirs for their own selfish ends. Coal, oil, timber, minerals, the schools of fishes are all natural products of our great outdoors. I do not advocate that they should belong to the government, but the government should see to it that the men dealing with those resources should not gut them and not spoil the beauty and health-giving properties of the forests and rivers.*

—— Zane Grey

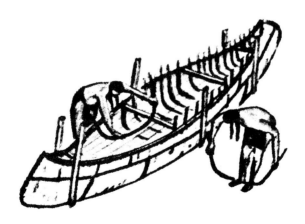

*Chippewa Canoe*

The native American has been generally despised by his white conquerors for his poverty and simplicity. They forget, perhaps, that his religion forbade the accumulation of wealth and the enjoyment of luxury. To him, as to other single-minded men in every age and race, from Diogenes to the brothers of St. Francis, from the Montanists to the Shakers, the love of possessions has appeared a snare, and the burdens of a complex society a source of needless peril and temptation. Furthermore, it was the rule of his life to share the fruits of his skill and success with his less fortunate brothers. Thus he kept his spirit free from the clog of pride, cupidity, or envy, and carried out, as he believed, the divine decree — a matter profoundly important to him . . .

—— "The Soul of the Indian"
Charles Alexander Eastman (Ohiyesa)
University of Nebraska Press

*Chippewa Quillwork on Birch Bark*

# Foreword

My wife Peggy saw Louis St. Germaine's obituary in the Chicago *Tribune* and immediately pointed it out to me. After reading it myself, we both had the same thought: Here is a man who should never be forgotten. Neither by those who knew and loved him nor by those who never had the chance to meet him in the flesh.

Having a branch of my family tree growing out of the Choctaw nation and traceable back through that blot on American history known as "The Trail of Tears," I pride myself on my own Indian heritage. I recall as a child of eight wishing to be of one blood, "a hundred per cent American," being my exact words to my third grade teacher. Nice lady that Mrs. Frey was, I don't believe she realized how much she hurt me at the time when she said that I could "never be a hundred per cent American."

It wasn't until I had grown into adulthood that I realized I am somewhat "more" American than those people who can't find an Indian in their ancestry. But I also came to the conclusion that I am not as "much" American as those people who still call themselves Native Americans or Indians.

With further maturity and study of the culture from which I had sprung, I came to realize that being "one hundred per cent American" is not a matter of blood lines. It is a condition of the heart. If you will, it is a spiritual feeling, possibly an emotion or a way of seeing the universe as being totally alive. Whatever you might call it, I felt I shared it with Louis St. Germaine and just as he might have wanted it, I wished to share it with everyone and everything.

In this day when we seem to be short of heroes and long on villains, in this age when we still suffer from bigotry of all kinds, I felt it was necessary that the whole world should know of this man named Louis St. Germaine. As Jerry Loar put it, " . . . he walked his way through all societies, economic brackets and ethnic groups." As I see him, race, creed, color, origin or whatever meant nothing to Louis St. Germaine. He saw with his heart, a rare gift.

But Louis St. Germaine was gone, a loss but not forever. Of course, his spirit would live in that plane of existence beyond this one, but I felt it should also live on in this realm. His spirit is so badly needed here, and I hoped that a book about Louis St. Germaine just might help keep his spirit among us. A grand ideal, no doubt, but ideals as well as pragmatic ideas make the world a better place.

With that intention, I searched for an author for this biography of Louis St. Germaine and found Tom Hollatz by telephone. I knew nothing of him at the time except that the local librarian had recommended him when I inquired about writers in the Minocqua area. On blind faith, I offered Tom a contract to do this book, and much to my surprise, he accepted. Something told me I had "done good."

As time went by between our initial conversation, exchange of letters, and the signing of the contracts, what little business sense I have began to nag at me, and I wondered if I had made a wise business decision in proposing this book and not only offering to publish it but also signing legal papers confirming the proposition.

Then I received Tom's manuscript. I read it. I read it again. I came to know Louis St. Germaine. My first inclinations — to have this book written and to publish it for all the world to have the same opportunity as I had — were proven beyond a doubt to be correct.

It is my only wish that you, the reader, share this feeling with me after reading the story of Louis St. Germaine, the life of Louis No. 1.

—— *Larry D. Names*
*Publisher*

# Introduction

The fishing guides of the Northwoods are a rare breed. They are independent, great storytellers, and for the most part, they know how to catch fish.

I have always been fascinated by the early tales of the guides and the stories they told. As a boy, the late Porter "Barefoot" Dean of Boulder Junction, Wis., could hold me in a spell for hours when he would tell me about the ones that didn't get away.

But there was one name, Louis St. Germaine of Lac du Flambeau, who generated respect from his peers, both Indian and non-Indian guides. He was known as "Louis No. 1" or "Big Louis". His ability as an athlete, fisherman, hunter, and guide placed him in an exceptional class. He fished with such names as Pres. Dwight D. Eisenhower, Pres. Harry S Truman, Gypsy Rose Lee, Bing Crosby as well as many of the top business leaders in the U.S. His good fishing friend was the great baseball star Ted Williams. Both were at the top of their professions when they got together to fish the waters of the Northwoods. When Williams heard of the death of Louis No. 1, he sent a touching letter about his friend which is included in these pages.

Louis St. Germaine touched so many lives with his quiet wit and an almost spiritual respect for the Northwoods. The following pages include conversations with those who knew him. He was truly a magician when it came to catching fish. Louis No. 1 was a class act. His legend lives . . .

—— Tom Hollatz
Boulder Junction, Wis.

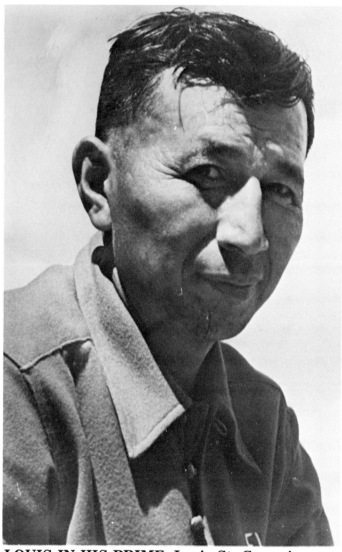

**LOUIS IN HIS PRIME.** Louis St. Germaine was born on the Lac du Flambeau Indian Reservation in northern Wisconsin in 1898. He grew up on the reservation and became a famous athlete and a legendary fishing guide.

# 1
# The Beginning of a Legend

*The ones who live are the ones who struggle.*
*The ones whose soul*
*and heart are filled with high purpose.*
*Yes, these are the living ones.*

—— Victor Hugo

A November wind was a razor cutting to the bone of the inhabitants of the Wisconsin Northwoods.

The trees were now barren of leaves except for the stingy brown oak leaves, which always drop to the earth in spring. Blue-gray clouds muscled their way across the Lac du Flambeau Indian reservation as an Indian mother hugged her two boys she soon would leave in a tiny cabin on the shore of White Sand Lake. Their father stood at the door, silently. No emotion colored his rugged Indian face.

"Be strong, my sons," she said softly as tears creased her face. "Louis, be strong. Take care of your brother."

At the age of nine, Louis St. Germaine was abandoned along with his brother on the shore of White Sand Lake. The only food left by his parents was a barrel of flour.

The baptism of young Louis into the real world

began on that cold November day. It was the beginning of a legend.

The forests of the Northwoods were filled with immense tall groves of pine. In some areas in the Lac du Flambeau area, the forests abound with oak, elm, basswood, walnut, hickory, butternut, slippery elm, poplar, sassafras, and dogwood. Other parts are filled with sugar maple, beech, birch, ash, hemlock, and ironwood. In low, swampy ground grow spruce, firs of various species, willow, alder, water ash, bird's-eye maple, cedar, larch, and sycamore. The wild fruit trees include several kinds of wild plums, crab apple, thorn, cherry, elder, and bush cranberry. Louis grew in the knowledge of his surroundings. He adapted it to survival.

He knew that many of the smaller lakes yielded plentiful supplies of wild rice, which when gathered in the autumn makes a wonderful soup. He soon learned that the woods and open areas yielded blackberries, huckleberries, strawberries, raspberries, gooseberries, black currants, wild grapes, and marsh cranberries. He also discovered a root that resembled in shape and taste a sweet potato.

It was during that first year — 1908 — that Louis learned that the lakes of the forests also were to harvest. The fish provided "meat" or protein, a life substance. And they were delicious. He also became quite good at catching fish, a skill that would enhance his legend throughout his life.

He also learned during the first summer alone in the world — 1909 — that catching fish was a way to earn money. Louis would haul his catch of the day to a nearby logging camp, where the loggers would reward him with money. It soon became a game — the more fish Louis caught the more money he would make.

His contact with the strong loggers was rich earth for the young oak. The original lumberjack was most colorful. Red was his color, the color in the wools that kept his muscled body from the biting cold of midwinter's frigid blasts. Years later when Louis formed the Flambeau Guides Association, the color he selected for all of the fishing guides was red. The socks too were a fiery red. Wool, Louis learned early, kept the cold from his body and was quick to dry. Many a time the young Louis and his brother, Charles, would fall through the ice while testing a not-yet-frozen lake.

Many times the true French logger in Lac du Flambeau wore a colorful sash about his waist. With a jack-knife, he severed his heavy woolen trousers just below the knee to make them "stagged" and more convenient for logging operations, especially on the rivers.

Although the great logging era of the Northwoods was on the downswing, the forests were still filled with loggers. Louis met and sold fish to French-Canadians, Scandinavians, Scots, Irish, and New Englanders. It was in these early days Louis learned to blend into many ways of life.

Louis also learned that the loggers who labored in winter bore pent-up thirsts that could only be quenched with winter wages. He saw how quickly a few drinks empowered biceps and fists to distribute "delightful black-eyes to the general public," according to Ivan Clyde Lake in his 1931 book, *Minocqua*. Lake added that the lumberjacks were the children of their time. In an untamed wilderness, they pitted their strength against the forces of Nature that must be conquered. Their very lives depended upon keenness of mind and quickness of body, a fact that the young Louis St. Germaine stored in his brain. Nature would win the struggle for mastery, or they. The disappearance of the virgin trees advertised their victory, and the lords of lumberdom for whom they labored grew rich.

That same fall, with a new dollar bulging in his pocket from a recent fish sale to the loggers, Louis and his brother walked to Minocqua in search of a treat. Little did they know that early morning what drama was about to unfold.

Just as they arrived in Minocqua, an explosion rocked the frame buildings of the downtown area. A "trio of strangers" blew up the safe in John Schilling's

Bank of Minocqua. Louis grabbed Charles and moved quickly to the nearby entrance of the hardware store. Their four wide, young Indian eyes watched as the three gunmen moved silently through the few towns-people who were awakened by the blast.

The three desperadoes took a nearby railway hand-car and headed south toward Hazelhurst. A team of horses, hauling officers to the nearby logging village, tried in vain to overtake them on the tracks but did reach Hazelhurst ahead of them. When the surprised trio arrived, shots were fired. No one was hit, and the bandits fled to the nearby woods, never to be apprehended.

Louis and Charles left Minocqua for the peace and quiet of the forest, wondering about their day in the white man's world.

Louis' old friend, Albert Cobe, tried to convince Louis to seek higher education. "I told him if I could do it, so could he. Louis never finished high school. The only college classes he could get were at Carlisle Indian School in Pennsylvania."

Louis was plucked from the woods when he was still a boy and sent to the government school in Lac du Flam-beau. It was another name for a jail. School sounded better. Louis spoke no English. It was there where Louis and the other Indian children would have the "Indian beaten out of them" if they failed to learn English quickly.

According to Albert Cobe, "Police would come a-round and pick you up and take you to school." Cobe said Indian youths would be whipped for running away. They would also be subjected to army-like lineups, inspections, and harsh punishments designed to quash any hint of Indian language and especially the rich Chippewa culture.

In the harshness, Louis learned how to play sports. It was that sports spark that would bring him fame far and wide as a great athlete.

Cobe: "His primary interest was sports. All Indians at the time were interested in sports . . . we never had any coaching. We learned by doing."

The 6'2" Cobe was the center on the Flambeau basketball team, which also included Louis. "Anyone who could walk or run played baseball," said Cobe.

"St. Germaine was wiry and strong," Cobe remembers. "He was an inspiration to us all because he was always in great shape. I told the other boys to look up to him. See how good he is. I'd tell them Louis didn't smoke or drink and that's the reason he's so good."

What might have been in the world of athletics is fun to think about. Louis knew the great Olympic medalist Jim Thorpe at Carlisle Insitute. Cobe is convinced that Louis would have become equally famous with Thorpe, but Louis left college in his first year, never to return. Cobe said, "He wanted to play baseball as soon as winter ended."

Perhaps the end of Louis' college career ended before it started. Pennsylvania is a long way from Lac du Flambeau. His very spirit lived there. It could not be moved.

"You've got to remember," said Cobe, a former teacher, "Indian children were not encouraged to go to school. I never knew I had any ability until I saw it on a transcript from Haskell College. I took that record to a Social Security office. The fellow there said, 'Hey, you must be a smart boy. Look at these grades.' I asked him, 'What makes you think so?' and he said, 'You got straight A's in math.' "

The early trail of Louis in the Lac du Flambeau area has been covered by time. It is a testimony to his life that he moved so quietly, letting his deeds do the talking for him. Sigurd Olson wrote, "Simplicity in all things is one of the secrets of the wilderness." The simplicity of Louis, too, was one of his secrets.

# Kinfolk remember 'Big Louie,' ace guide

By WILLIAM SISSON

When fishing for the elusive muskellunge, Louis St. Germaine would wear dark colored clothes, a forest green shirt perhaps, so as not to spook the keen and wary quarry.

He would also keep his tackle box closed, his hooks sharp, his hands out of the water and his fishing rod working.

Others would do well following the practices of St. Germaine, "Big Louie," or "Louis No. 1," as he was known around Wisconsin's Lac du Flambeau area. He was one of the truly great fishing guides of this century.

St. Germaine, a Chippewa Indian who guided such famous sportsmen as Ted Williams, died recently from cancer. He was 84.

Fisherman, athlete, hunter, guide and conservationist, St. Germaine drew clients from across the country, some of whom he guided for 40 years or more. He took close friends fishing on a limited basis until

ally found either alone or in groups up to three. The large, cautious fish are strong fighters requiring anglers to use heavy freshwater tackle and large lures. As a rule, many hours of casting go into hooking one of the toothy "freshwater barracudas."

St. Germaine and his parties boated several muskie weighing more than 50 pounds and many more in the 30- to 40-pound range. Several of the larger muskies that once hung in a local tavern referred to as the "muskie bar" were taken by St. Germaine.

"He had what we call the touch," said Harold "Tuffy" Titus, who was the only white person playing on the Flambeau Indian basketball team coached by St. Germaine. The coach affectionately referred to Titus as son. "They're still talking about him up here."

"He was a super muskie man," said Tom Hollatz, an

author who is writing a book on the guide. "That was his forte. When Ted Williams used to fish up here in the 1940s, Louis St. Germaine was his favorite guide. When you're fishing with Ted Williams, you're a pretty classy act."

St. Germaine, a perfectionist when it came to fishing, fashioned his own muskie lures. His brother used to drag the lures through the water and St. Germaine would swim beneath the surface to evaluate their action and determine how to improve it.

"He was the cream of the crop," said Hollatz. "He's the stuff legends are made of."

"He was known as a good muskie man," said Jerry Loar, president of Dillman's Sand Lake Lodge. St. Germaine guided out of the Loar lodge for more than 50 years. "He'd throw muskie plugs for eight or 10 hours a day."

St. Germaine fished hundreds

of lakes both on and off the reservation. He could read a lake, even a strange one, as easily as one reads the morning paper.

"He was uncanny at remembering the locations of fish," said Loar. If St. Germaine spotted a muskie following his lure but couldn't coax it into hitting, he would make a mental note of the spot and return another day.

Above all else, Loar respected St. Germaine's ability to cut across ethnic and economic barriers. "If all the people in the world were like Louis St. Germaine," he said, "there would be no tribal or race problems."

St. Germaine treated the woods and lakes with respect. Because he was an Indian, he had the right to spear fish on the reservation. But he never did nor did he allow his sons to. "He was a great one for conservation," said William St.

Germaine. "He'd never break the law."

Arthur "Bud" Knudtson, a retired state conservation warden, remembers St. Germaine as a professional guide.

"In my many years here as a conservation officer," said Knudtson, "I never had one complaint on him. Not one. He was a very strong, very independent and very conservation-minded."

That never changed, not even during his illness. "He never complained," said Florence Allen. During his last nine days, he refused all food and water. "He took nothing, nothing. It was his wish," she said. "The doctors couldn't get over it."

Big Louie, who taught children and stars alike to fish, died March 12.

# 2
# His Four Children
# Remember Their Father

*Virtuous and wise he was, but not severe;*
*He still remember'd that he once was young.*
—— Art of Preserving Health
John Armstrong, 1709-1779

To know Louis, we recalled his memory through his
four children — Margaret Lilly, Flossie Allen, and
Richard and William St. Germaine. All display a pride
in their Indian heritage and have an unmatched air of
confidence and poise.

William, the oldest son, lives in Lac du Flambeau
and continues to be a top fishing guide. The youngest
son, Richard, is a supervisor for International Con-
struction Co. He was recently in Zaire, Africa, and later
was sent to a remote island in the Aleutians.

Margaret, presently of Lac du Flambeau, is the
former manager of the Red Carpet Exposition Center
in Milwaukee. Her husband is a former supervisor on
the Apollo space program. The youngest daughter,
Flossie Allen, is a counselor in Lac du Flambeau with
the Indian Child Welfare, Family Service and Child

Placement office. Her Husband, Willis, is manager of the Lac du Flambeau fish hatchery.

We thank them for helping us recall a marvelous father and human being, Louis St. Germaine.

Louis survived his brothers and a sister.

His sister, Florence, was dying of tuberculosis in Kansas. Louis wanted to be with her at the end. He left Lac du Flambeau and headed southwest toward Kansas, hitchhiking all the way. When Florence saw Louis, she smiled and was at peace. She soon died, and Louis trudged back to the Northwoods.

Charles, who was abandoned with Louis on the shore of White Sand Lake, died a tragic death. He was entertaining Louis and a friend by hopping from log to log in a hot pond. Suddenly, Charles lost his balance and tumbled under the logs, which were on their way to the sawmill. The logs kept his young body submerged, and before Louis could reach him, Charles was dead. The sadness of that loss carved a new line in Louis' granite face.

Louis buried his brother Milton and Milton's son Milan at the same time in Lac du Flambeau. Milan was killed in Italy during World War II after he wiped out a German machine-gun nest with a hand grenade. He sacrificed his life for his Army buddies. Milton died a natural death in the Northwoods, and they were buried together.

Perhaps the most tragic of all the St. Germaine deaths was the drowning death of Joe.

Joe, also a fishing guide of reknown, was guiding two men in his canoe. A buck deer was swimming across the lake and for some reason struck the canoe, flipping its occupants into the cold, crystal clear water. All three men drowned. One body was found, but Joe and the other fisherman were still missing.

"Dad was told to go see this medicine man, Johnson," Flossie said. "He was also told to bring some tobacco. He did, and when he went there, the old fellow was sitting outside of his wigwam. 'I've been waiting for you,' said the medicine man. Dad offered him the tobacco. The man drew a picture of a lake on the ground. Although one man was found, the medicine man marked the spots where all the bodies were. He said one of the men would be found standing up on the bottom of the lake holding onto a paddle. He was found that way."

Billy (William) added, "They even dynamited the lake trying to find the bodies before my dad visited the medicine man."

Flossie concluded the story, saying, "The medicine man said Joe was under a log. He marked the exact location, and that's where my dad found him."

Margie told us about her mother and her family and how she met Louis. "My mother was Irish and German. They (her family) moved to Antigo after the Civil War. Their family plantation was lost. They were a very wealthy family and lost everything after the war. . . . My mother owned a boarding house in Antigo. Mom, who was very beautiful, was walking down the street with the man she was going to marry. Dad just walked between them and nudged him out of the way. She was smitten with his athletic prowess."

Richard recalls what a vital and vigorous man his father was. "Dad was very active all his life. I remember he came to California to live with me for a while. He loved to work. Always wanted a list of things to do. Then he would stay. He had to be doing something."

Billy remembers a special time with his father in the outdoors. "I hated potatoes. My dad was going to teach me to eat potatoes. We went camping for five days with no food, just potatoes. He forgot one thing. He taught me how to survive in the woods on acorns, wintergreen berries, raspberries, hazelnuts, but I never ate a potato. He taught me too good about the woods. And you know that today I love potatoes."

Billy learned the art of fishing from his dad. He would often accompany him when he guided only one person. Finally, when Billy started guiding, Louis said, "You're on your own. No one taught me how to fish." Billy was a good guide too and fished out of Dillman's.

Louis liked to fish with bucktails and suicks.

Billy added, "He liked to tell stories on the water. Always kept a straight face while telling you lies."

"One day he was fishing with Bing Crosby. He loved to tell this story. They were fishing for walleyes, and Crosby kept losing walleyes. Now the secret of catching walleyes is to wait and then set the hook. He got Bing singing all day. Each time a walleye hit he would tell Bing to sing one stanza of *Auld Lang Syne* before setting the hook. It worked. Crosby became a good walleye fisherman."

Louis loved his family. He would take them to many events including the sports shows in Milwaukee. One day he took them to an animal display at one of the midwinter shows. A teacher was telling a group of her pupils that wolves hated Indians as she pointed at a live wolf in a cage. Louis walked up to the cage, put out his hand, and the wolf licked it. Color one teacher's face red.

Native Americans – Indians – were forbidden to drink in their native land. Billy tells the following story:

"One day my dad was fishing with Senator Bob LaFollette. They went up to Little Bohemia. Emil Wanatka, the owner, knew my dad and would allow him to drink at the bar. As a joke, they wouldn't serve LaFollette and made him sit in the kitchen. LaFollette really got a kick out of that. He laughed about it all the time."

Billy related how Louis played no favorites about who he guided on fishing trips. "My dad fished with everyone from crooks to politicians. He knew Ralph and Al Capone." (Ralph had a summer home in nearby Mercer, Wisconsin, where Al was a frequent guest.)

The family also remembered the time Big Louis was fishing with two well-known "notorious crooks." The two mixed martinis in a minnow bucket in the boat. The lead from the walls of the pail corrupted that perfect elixir and both took sick. Louis, who did not drink booze, rushed both of the gangsters to the hospital where their stomachs were pumped.

Louis also saved several persons involved in a two-boat accident. One of the boats flipped sending fishermen floundering in the lake. Louis jumped into the water and held both boats and dragged them to a shallow sand bar on Sand Lake. He knew he couldn't get them to shore in the high wind. The wind ripped at the boats, but Louis held fast. The power of the wind and the weight of the boats broke several of his ribs, yet he held tight until help came.

Gypsy Rose Lee, the famous striptease artiste, was one of Louis' customers. Billy tells about the time Louis took her fishing. "Dad was a funny guy, especially where women were concerned. One day after guiding Gypsy Rose Lee, she invited my dad into the bar at the resort where she was staying. He refused to go in because of her foul mouth."

Flossie added, "I never heard Dad swear. Ever. Only once. It was in a hospital. He told one of the nurses to leave him alone. He swore then, but it wasn't bad."

Gypsy Rose Lee was a friend of Mrs. Robert Uihlein, the Schlitz lady who owns several lakes and acres-upon-acres of land in Land O'Lakes. Louis couldn't stand the famed stripper, but he did enjoy the grace and class of Mrs. Uihlein. He wouldn't take Gypsy out again, but he was always proud to take out "the beer lady."

Louis' love of children, too, is the thing legends are made of. Billy related, "He would always discourage drinking and smoking by his players. One day a young man named Rusty came to the game loaded. He begged my dad to let him play. Dad said no but finally changed his mind. 'Okay,' he said, 'go out there and make a fool of yourself.' Rusty did. He dropped the ball and fell on the floor. Dad didn't take him out of the game and let Rusty make a fool out of himself. Everytime my dad would see him after that, he would laugh."

When the family got together to remember Louis on March 17, 1983, Margie told the following story:

"We were having a party. The Aschenbreners who owned the hardware store brought the beer. It was truly a fun party. There was laughter and good times. Louis, too, had a ball. The following year Louis had to be at his job at the Elgin Academy. The party was a bomb. We sat like stones. Nothing. It was evident that Louis was the spark of the party. He would always get people to do things. It wasn't the same without him."

Janet Blair, a reporter who talked with the family, said, "It sounded like he was a catalyst . . . in fact he is a catalyst today as we sit and talk about him . . . it was my dad who said you're not gone as long as we're remembered."

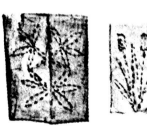

*Chippewa Birch Bark Transparencies*

A GOOD CATCH. Louis St. Germaine (center) and two grateful customers display a nice stringer of walleyes at Armour Lake Resort in Presque Isle, Wis. Although he loved to fish the Flambeau chain, Louis also liked to fish the waters of the Presque Isle-Boulder Junction area.

# BASKET BALL

## THURS. JAN. 1, 1925

### Laona City Team
vs.

### Antigo Athletics

You have all heard of, or seen Louis St. Germaine the smooth Indian player. He will be here and have a bunch with him that play fancy basketball. Come out and see our boys fight to win.

### At the High School Gymnasium
At 7:30 P. M. Standard Time

Admission

**AN INVITATION TO EXCITEMENT.** Posters such as this one were tacked to every available space when Louis St. Germaine was coming to town to play basketball. Although Louis' "home" team was the Lac du Flambeau Indians, reknowned sports enthusiast Jimmy Ford told the story of how Louis played for just about everyone at one time or another. The reason? Ticket sales. When folks heard Louis St. Germaine would be on the visiting team, they turned out in droves. Jimmy Ford said he was impressed with Louis the first time he saw him play, but he was more impressed when he saw Louis play the second time against him — but with another team. Louis was what folks used to call a "ringer."

# 3
# The Athlete

*Is it so small a thing*
*To have enjoy'd the sun,*
*To have lived light in the spring,*
*To have loved, to have thought, to have done;*
*To have advanced true friends . . .*
—— Empedocles on Etna
Matthew Arnold

Louis stayed in the North and grew with grace and style. His athletic ability began to soar like an eagle.

The Green Bay Packers basketball team scheduled games against his team. Teams were booked from everywhere. The Gold Coast Booking agency, 812 W. Walnut St., Milwaukee, Wisconsin, sent a postcard asking for a game.*

*Dear Sir: I have a colored basketball team that*
*goes by the name of the Harlem Aces. My terms are*

* Author's note: As I read the old postcard dated Nov. 6, 1941 and spotted the address — 812 W. Walnut St., Milwaukee — my mouth dropped. When I was attending college in that great city in 1959, I lived off campus. The house I lived in was 812 W. Walnut. Talk about Rod Serling time!

*the first $15 taken in and 50 percent of the remaining gross gate or $40 guarantee. I will send you 15 posters to help sponsor the game. Name your own date. Please answer. S.E. Dowell.*

The posters from the time Louis played stated words like: *Louis St. Germaine, the smooth Indian player.* Another read: *St. Germaine, the fast Indian floor man.*

Margie, Louis' oldest daughter, is the only member of the family who saw him play. She remembered his agility and quickness. "He was a fine ball handler. I got so excited at one of his games that I wanted to stand up and lead cheers.

"I remember one day that the coach and my father were loading a stationwagon, and he hit his eye on the corner of the wagon. He would try to make humor out of everything. He told me, 'Margie, I can see my ear.' His eye was hanging out. It turned out okay."

Louis was the only member of his family that never wore glasses. His eye healed well. When he died, he left his eyes to the Eye Bank. The fish still aren't safe. Somewhere there is a fisherman with Louis' eyes.

Louis and his Lac du Flambeau Indians were big news in the '20s. It was a day without television. Only squeaky radios provided any mass media entertainment. Imagine mom and pop taking the kids to see magical Indian ballplayers who could do everything with a basketball except make it disappear.

One headline read:

**Late Arrangement
Is Made for Game
Louis St. Germaine to Show
His Bag of Tricks Here
Tonight**

The main sports story read in part:
*. . . St. Germaine, the tricky Indian of the Antigo squad, will give what is worth the admission alone. Playing here*

April 13, 1983

Mr. Tom Hollatz
Bear Lodge
Box 100, Rt. 1
Boulder Junction, WI 54512

Dear Tom:

Just a few words about my remembrances of Louis St. Germaine.

I started to fish up in Wisconsin with a very distinguished group of men and we stayed at Green Lake. There was a Dutchman who ran it (I can't remember his name) - a very nice place. I was introduced to Louis St. Germaine at that time; got to fish with him over a period of 3 or 4 years. He was recognized then as absolutely the best Muskie guide in that part of the country.

I remember distinctly one little trick he pulled on me - one which I caught him at. As you may know, he used a pool cue as a fishing rod. He certainly believed in a stout rod and a strong line because in those days, as even today, they used Zuick bait and it required a stiff rod to handle it.

One of his tricks with somebody who was new in the boat, when they were not looking, was to make a helluva splash right by the boat, like it had been a Muskie following the bait and of course, that would shake up the angler.

I can't tell you how bad I feel to hear the sad news, but I know he had a wonderful, full life and probably spent more hours fishing for Muskie than anyone I've ever known.

Kindest regards to all.

Sincerely,

*Ted Williams*

Ted Williams

TW/shg

**A FRIEND REMEMBERS.** Baseball Hall-of-Famer Ted Williams was a close friend of Louis St. Germaine's. They shared many good times together in the Northwoods, memories that Williams will always cherish. As his letter to the author states, he was very saddened by Louis' death but accepted it philosophically, knowing that Louis had no regrets.

last year, St. Germaine delighted fans by his movement, holding the ball with one hand, in the crotch of his arm and in other ways that bewildered the Ironwood organization.

Manager Backon was able to book the Indian squad because the Indians heard the Legion unit was making a good showing and Antigo didn't want to go back home without two scalps when the opportunity was presented.

Another newspaper heralded Louis' overwhelming presence on the court.

. . . *Big Chief Smile-on-the-Face St. Germaine and four other Indian braves almost made Ironwood take a back seat in basket ball last night.*

It was a game that the Indian team lost in overtime, a rare occasion.

## Basket
## Ball
## Thurs. Jan. 1, 1925
## Laona City Team
## vs.
## Antigo Athletics

*You have all heard of, or seen Louis St. Germaine the smooth Indian player. He will be here and have a bunch with him that play fancy basket ball. Come out and see our boys fight to win.*

*At the High School Gymnasium*
*At 7:30 p.m. Standard time*
*Admission .............20 cents and 35 cents*

Another poster alerted enthusiastic fans that Louis No. 1 was coming on Friday, January 12.

## Basket Ball
## Smetana's Hall
## Fri., Jan. 12
## Langlade Co. Normal Team
## vs.

## Deerbrook A.A.

*This promises to be an exceptionally good game, with the winner hard to pick. Deerbrook has been greatly strengthened by the addition of St. Germaine, the fast Indian floor man.*

*Game called 8.00 p.m. Admission, 15 cents and 25 cents*

*Everybody's Going!*

The sports writing is vintage and almost laughable by today's standards.

*. . . Smile-on-the-face Louis pegged one from near the center of the floor. It bobbled a bit and dropped in the net.*

*. . Band-Around-the-Head Peter now took a turn at shooting a long one and it never touched the ring . . .*

Louis, who at times played forward on the Antigo team, received other favorable press notices.

*. . . He is one of the shiftiest players the game has seen in action. And best of all, no player plays the game in a more sportsmanlike manner than St. Germaine . . .*

Louis played on the Minocqua city team from 1930 to 1936. Les Rusch, a teammate and a Minocqua town supervisor, remembers Louis well.

"He was quick like a cat," Les said. "He wasn't much of a shooter. None of us were. But could he pass a ball." Rusch added that in "those days" for a player to score six or even four points was a big deal.

"We won about three-quarters of our games with Louis," said Rusch who played forward on the team. "He was a true magician. You had to watch him every moment. He would pass under his legs and under the legs of an opponent. That usually brought applause from the crowd."

When Louis played, crowds jammed the gym of the Minocqua community center which was constructed in 1927.

"You couldn't believe it," said Rusch. "There was a wedge of people at each end of the court crowding onto the floor just to watch Louis play. It was incredible.

Remember in those days we had no television. Basketball was our entertainment."

The famous Harlem Globetrotters payed a visit to Minocqua to face St. Germaine and his teammates, including Rusch, Floyd Mullendore, Earl Fredrickson, Harold Kumrow, Larry Hirsch, and Lawrence Bradley.

"And we beat the 'Trotters," boasted Rusch. "We really gave it to them, and Louis was his fabulous self. Well, they came back that same year. This time we lost."

Rusch and St. Germaine remained friends after the sporting days. They would often eat together in Milwaukee during the winter months. "He had a tremendous personality. It was a likeable grin he always wore on his face."

Rusch placed Louis in the top bracket as a fishing guide along with the famous Jim Kennedy of the Minocqua chain. "They both were terrific," said the Minocqua native.

Harold Titus of Minocqua, known as "Tuffy" to his friends, said, "He always called me son." Like St. Germaine, Titus was a sensational athlete. He, too, could do it all: basketball, baseball, and football. At one time, he was the only white man on the Flambeau Indian basketball team in 1939 and 1940. Louis was the coach.

"Louis' wife was a redhead," Titus related. "I believe she was Irish and German. One day when we were playing baseball and someone asked Louis why there was a white kid on the Indian baseball team, Louis said, 'He's my son,' while pointing at his white wife.

"Louis was a marvelous man. He loved humor, and he could be serious." Lac du Flambeau was a sports Mecca in its day. Titus added, "There was a tremendous baseball field with 500 seats and a fence. It was first class. People would come from everywhere, including Wausau to watch the great Indian teams. Whenever they played some of the great colored teams, there was standing-room-only crowds."

St. Germaine also played baseball at times with the

Yellowjackets, a pro team from Minocqua. Teams in those days would invite players from other area teams to bolster their rosters when a good team would be coming, a practice commonly known as "bringing in a ringer." Such visiting teams included the likes of the scandalous 1919 Chicago White Sox, often referred to as the Chicago "Black Sox."

According to Titus, Louis' daughter Flossie always resembled an "Indian princess" in her youth. "She was one of the most beautiful girls ever to be born in Lac du Flambeau." While acting as a pallbearer at Louis' funeral, Titus saw Flossie with her back turned to him. He walked up behind her as quietly as he could, put his hands over her eyes, kissed her, and said, "Bet you can't guess who this is." Ever so softly, she replied, "Hello, brother."

Tuffy Titus had a few things to say about Louis' athletic ability. "You couldn't believe it. Not only Louis, but all those great Indian players could do everything the Harlem Globetrotters did. They could spin the ball on their fingers. Pass behind their backs. Everything!"

Flossie said, "I remember one time in Wausau. The fans were going to kill him because he was so good. He was in the washroom, and they wanted to get him. Finally, the police came and helped him. They escorted him out of town. People were mad because he won the game."

Billy related, "Another time he had to escape from a wash room window. The crowd was mad at him."

Some of the Harlem Globetrotters, including Goose Tatum, Meadowlark Lemon, and the team's founder, the late Abe Saperstein, visited the St. Germaine home. Saperstein once invited the Flambeau Indians to play on the road, but none of them wanted to leave the reservation.

Recalling a trip to Antigo with the Indian basketball team, Titus said, "We had three cars, all owned by the Indians. They were in terrible condition, really awful shape, but we headed out anyway. After a few miles, we stopped, and all of the Indians got out and ran to one of the cars. I couldn't see what they were doing. Again we took off, and some 15 miles later we stopped by the side of the road again. The Indians went to one of the cars, opened the trunk, and finally returned to the cars. The next time we stopped I decided to see what they were doing and got out with them. I couldn't believe it. In each trunk, there were many old bald tires. They looked like tires that people would throw away. It seems every 15 miles or so one of the tires on the cars would go flat, and they simply put on an old bald tire to replace the flat one. This ritual continued to and from the basketball games, but it was fun. Louis would just smile and take it all in stride."

Jim Ford, noted sports authority and the Durkee food company's "Spice King", played against Louis on the basketball court. Ford, a star player for Green Bay West High School in 1934, toured with the Green Bay Packers basketball team. The team was made up of players who wanted to keep in shape during the winter months as well as promote the football team around the state of Wisconsin and the Upper Peninsula of Michigan.

"In 1935-36," said Ford, "the Packers were barnstorming all the towns of Wisconsin. That touring team included the likes of Arnie Herber, George Sauer, Buckets Goldenberg, and Johnny Blood, to name a few of the Packer greats. They too were in awe of 'The Indian' Louis No. 1.

"He was everywhere," Ford recalled during an interview in the Little Minocqua Motel. "It seems in every town we played, St. Germaine was on the opposing team. He was so in demand by those teams that it was incredible. Louis was a gifted athlete. Truly outstanding. If I could compare him to anyone, it would be to Meadowlark Lemon of the Harlem Globetrotters. Louis was never a show-off or anything like that, but he was truly gifted. Louis was really born 20 years too soon. He would have been a marvelous star in the NBA (National Basketball Association).

"But I never got to meet Louis socially until 1938," said Ford, who played second base and shortstop with the highly competitive Minocqua city baseball team. "It was John Ames, Sr., who introduced me to him. 'At last,' I said to Louis, 'we get to meet.'"

Ford, who at one time was the property of the Boston Red Sox and a scout with the Pittsburgh Pirates, said it was St. Germaine who invented the behind-the-back pass in the game basketball. "He could do it all. He was really something to watch." Ford also said Louis would impede the progress of a player by "hooking his pants with his finger. He never cracked a smile when he did it, but he was clever. When I think back to Louis, he was in a class by himself . . . a great athlete."

Ben Guthrie, a Lac du Flambeau town officer for 26 years, knew Louis well, playing on the same basketball team with him in the 1930s.

"It was always fun to play with Louis," said Guthrie, who owned the popular Fireside in Lac du Flambeau for years. "He was very tricky, always making the game fun. I really don't think he took the game seriously."

Guthrie, who played semi-pro ball as a "running guard" on Louis' team, jumped center on the team because of his height.

Mrs. Agnes Valliere remembers Louis for his pride. "He was a very popular man," she said in the kitchen of her son Hiram's home. "He was always proud he was an Indian. He loved his Indian heritage but did like the white man's ways. I remember seeing him play basketball in Green Bay one night. He made a shot from half court, and he scored. I'd say he was shy around people. If people asked, he would always sign an autograph. As early as 1919, people just knew he was a basketball magician."

Hiram, a builder, recalled the court exploits of Louis. "You can't say enough about his dribbling. Spectacular was the only word for it. His behind-the-back passes were fantastic. People talk about Larry Bird's[*] passing. Louis was in that class."

\* The All-Pro forward of the Boston Celtics.

**A FRIENDLY SALUTE.** Well known sports enthusiast Jimmy Ford knew Louis St. Germaine personally, and he played against Louis in both basketball and baseball. "I'd heard about Louis before I played against him," Ford said. "And after playing against him, I found out what everyone was saying was true. He was a great athlete. But when I played against him the second time, he was playing for a different team. And so it went. No matter who we were playing, Louis was always there playing against us. He was so popular with the fans that if you wanted to sell a lot of tickets you hired Louis to play for you.

A SLICK PLAYER. In his playing days, Jimmy Ford was a standout at second base and shortstop on the baseball diamond and a quick guard on the basketball court. He played baseball in the Boston Red Sox organization and was later a scout for the Pittsburgh Pirates.

While showing me some beautiful woodcarvings by Bill Valliere, Hiram added, "Louis was respected by the white community, too. In those days, Indians were barred from drink. Many places would allow Louis to drink at the bar. It was on August 15, 1953 when the 83rd Congress passed Public Law 280 that Indians could drink legally."

Mrs. Valliere added, "I remember Louis encouraging us to walk and sit up straight in church. 'Why?' we asked him. He said, 'Pride.' "

Mike Aschenbrener knew Louis well. Mike organized eight Indian Basketball teams for the government.

"Louis was the coach, and I did the organizing," said Aschenbrener, whose collection of Lac du Flambeau memorabilia would put many a library and Indian museum to shame. "We had telegrams from Abe Saperstein pleading with us to take the Flambeau Indians on the road. Everything was all set. It's funny that we didn't take the offer. The reason? All of the wives and girlfriends would have to travel with us.

"Louis was masterful dribbler. It was an art form with him. He was in a class by himself. Many times we were left short-handed on the court when players fouled out. Louis and two others would continue to play and beat the full five-man squads."

The Flambeau Indians were also one of the first teams to score more than 100 points in a game. It was common for early basketball scores to be in the 20-19 or 22-16 range. The reasons: those medicine-ball-like leather basketballs; the jump-shot was in its embryo stage; and there was a center jump at mid-court after every basket.

As Aschenbrener showed me a gold-plated saxaphone, a gift from his friend Rudy Vallee, he said, "I remember one great high-scoring day. We played an afternoon game in Michigan, scoring over 100 points and later that night a game in Eagle River. 100 points again. For the two games, we scored some 240 points. Now, that's playing.

"It was in those days of St. Germaine's basketball antics that many times the crowds wanted more and more of Louis' talents. He was such a positive and an up person. Those crowds didn't want the game to end, and many times asked us to stay an extra quarter or two. They couldn't get enough of what they called 'those clever Indians.' And they got their money's worth."

Louis guided for the Aschenbreners at their Lake Shore Cottages on Big Crawling Stone Lake in Lac du Flambeau. "As a guide," said Aschenbrener, "there was none better."

Mike brought out another box of the treasured past of Lac du Flambeau. While pouring over the old papers and photos, Mike played a recording of the late Franklyn McCormick, a late-night personality on Chicago radio station WGN. The date was February 17, 1967. McCormick spoke in those deep, marvelous tones of his about the retirement from WGN of Carl J. Meyers, who savored every moment in his beautiful Lac du Flambeau. Many a night did Carl and yours truly swap Chicago *Tribune*-WGN stories while quaffing nondehydrating brews at Yeschek's Tower when Aschenbrener operated that marvelous restaurant.

I hated to leave Aschenbrener's colorful museum-like basement. For me, it was a wonderful walk down memory lane. It was an exciting trip.

*Chippewa Embroidered Moccasin*

**PICTURE THIS. In 1949, two top fishing guides of the Northwoods, Louis St. Germaine (left) and Jim Peck, were cover models for Mercury's new line of outboards.**

# 4

# The Fishing Guide

*As no man is born an artist,*
*so no man is born an angler.*

*It (angling) deserves commendations . . . it is an art,*
*and an art worthy the knowledge of a wise man.*

*Angling is somewhat like poetry,*
*men are to be born so.*
—— Compleat Angler. Epistle to the Reader
Izaak Walton

"He loved muskies more than anyone else," said another dynamic Northwoods fishing guide, Jim Peck, a friend of St. Germaine's for some 20 years. Peck hired Louis and other Indian guides for customers for his popular fishing camp on Fence Lake.

Peck moved to the Northwoods from Freeport, Ill., where he was a light-heavyweight boxer. Out of 48 fights, he only lost three. Today, Peck operates *Wildwood*, perhaps the finest wildlife farm in the United States. It is a spotless place and is located on Highway 70 in Minocqua. Peck is perhaps the most enthusiastic of all the Northwoods guides. When I talk to Jim, I always get the feeling that I'm talking with a cheerleader.

"Louis guided for me many years," said Peck. "He was a free-lancer." In addition to St. Germaine, Peck hired some 20 other Indian guides to handle 90 fishing guests. Along with Louis, other top guides out of Peck's were Big Ed Christiansen, Buck Christiansen, Stan Christiansen, Harry St. Germaine, and Eli Beson, to name a few.

"Louis was one of the hardest workers for muskies," said Peck. He'd row all day. A lot of the other Indian guides would just stay in one place, but Louis worked hard. He was always very loyal to me and my guests. He was a standout person. There was a lot of good about him. There was a great sense of pride about him. He always wore clean clothes."

Peck, who remains one of the top guides in the Northwoods, said, "Louis was my guide."

In 1949, Louis and Peck were cover models for the new line of Mercury motors. Peck said, "The film crew loved him. He was always kind and polite." Peck added that at the time the new Mercury models were top secret and the film crew actually hid the new design from his customers. "As soon as they were done shooting for the day, they'd put them back in their cases. They were light and beautiful motors."

Peck also starred in a major *Wausau Employers Insurance* ad campaign, appearing in spots during the CBS television network program *60 Minutes* catching a musky. That same campaign was used in a national magazine. He also appeared in a national campaign for the Miller Brewing Company, fixing a traditional shore lunch.

Peck, who has over 1,500 legal muskies to his credit, thought a moment about his friend, then said, "Louis was a handsome devil. He truly was a conservationist. Many a time Louis would come in with a few fish rather than hog a legal catch. He was very conservative when it came to fishing. Boy, he was a good one. Color him class."

One of the best guides of St. Germaine's era was

Harvey Bagley, now 84, of Boulder Junction, Wis., which is aptly nicknamed the "Musky Capital of the World."

Bagley, who also guided such notables as President Dwight D. Eisenhower when he was still a general in the Army and Hollywood actress Elizabeth Taylor, was highly respected as a fishing guide and as a human being.

Interviewed in his modest green log cabin home just off County Highway M in Boulder Junction, Bagley recalled the great Louis St. Germaine with affection.

"What a tremendous reputation!" he said. "Before I ever met him, I heard about this great Indian guide in Lac du Flambeau. He wasn't known for just one species, but he was good at whatever he went after. He truly tried to please his customers and really appreciated the tourist as an asset. He would get his limit and then get off the water. Even if a guest wanted to go out again for another species, Louis would always say no. I never knew many Indians, but Louis was someone I was proud to know."

Bagley was one of the better musky guides of the Northwoods. He always used "Skinner" spoons and liked feathers on his lures. When he used bucktails for muskies, he always placed two strips of red flannel on only two outer hooks of a trailing treble hook.

Another one of the master fishing guides of the Northwoods, Pop Dean of Sayner, Wis., knew Big Louis well and shared many an afternoon on the water with him.

"Louis was in a class by himself," said Dean. "He knew how to catch fish. He always liked to fish Clear and Little Trout Lakes and the waters of Manitowish Waters as well as the Flambeau chain.

"He was the first one to invent the flatfish lure. It was made out of moose wood. That was a shrub so high. It was like rubber. You could strip the bark all the way up from the base through the leaves. You'd take that 'rope' and tie it around deer antlers to haul the deer through the woods. Then Louis would take some of the pulp and bend it around a tree and tie it there. The next

**ANOTHER GREAT GUIDE. Nelson Sheppo of Lac du Flambeau is also a great Indian fishing guide. Sheppo displays one of the classiest collections of fishing poles and reels in the North. He became a gifted fishing guide thanks to the kindness of Louis St. Germaine, his friend.**

A FISHERMAN'S FISHERMAN. Howard "Pop" Dean of the Sayner-St. Germaine, Wisconsin area was another one of the fabled Northwoods' guides. Although he received less publicity than his brother Porter "Barefoot" Dean, Pop was a great fisherman in his own right. He, too, admired and respected Louis No. 1. When Maylin Ruff was asked to compare the two men as fishing guides, his reply was, "Don't ask me that." For those who knew Louis, that's how good Pop was, and for those who knew Pop but not Louis, that's how good Louis was. The fish were really in trouble when both men were on the same lake.

day it would be curved to make the flatfish lures. He put three single hooks on it. That was one of the first flatfish lures.

"Louis also made the first suick-like baits. The bait companies all learned from the Indians. They were master fishermen, and they knew what worked."

Pop Dean is the brother of the late Porter "Barefoot" Dean, a legendary fishing guide in his own right. Pop, like Louis, also guided a few famous persons in his 46 years on the water, including Jack Dempsey, Janet Gaynor, Ted Williams, Gen. Dwight D. Eisenhower, Don Ameche, Sen. Everett "Deerskin" Dirksen, and Charles Halleck, to name a few.

"The new guides are really something," said Dean. "They forget that an important part of guiding is the shore lunch. One young guide who has one of those fancy bass boats anchors his boat some 10 feet from the shore so his customer can watch the shore while he eats a sandwich and tastes some baked beans made on a gas stove in the boat. You mean to tell me that's a shore lunch?

"No part of the day is better than the shore lunch. It builds a lifetime of friendships. Your old guests know it's not the end of the world if you don't catch any fish on a particular day. It's the entire fishing experience, the friendship, that counts.

"I never got bored of fishing. Some of the newer guides don't realize that you learn something new everytime you hit the water."

Billy St. Germaine related the story of how one day Louis was guiding a party and two fishing poles came up missing. One of the men accused Louis of stealing the poles. Louis climbed into his 1937 Chevy and drove to town and bought them two new rods and reels and gave them to them. He then quit and refused to guide them ever again. Later the fishermen found the rods in the grass and apologized.

Margie added, "When he did give them the rods, he told them, 'Here, these are better than that dime store junk you had.' "

Long-time northern Wisconsin game warden Arthur "Bud" Knudtson knew Louis from the many times he encountered him on the water for license checks.

"He was a cherished fellow," said Knudtson. "He never complained and was always polite. Checked him one day on Clear Lake in the Manitowish chain. He had two people in the boat with him. He had a stringer chocked full of walleyes. Everytime I checked Louis, there was always a good stringer."

Knudtson, who worked from January 1946 to December 31, 1974 as a warden, admired St. Germaine, too, as a conservationist. "He never exploited anything. He took what was proper. What a tremendous man. It was a pleasure to know him."

Tom Newcomb of Boulder Junction, Wis., a superb walleye fishing guide in his own right, tells the following story about the always proper Louis:

"One day Louis was guiding a man and a woman. It also seemed Louis had a few internal combustion problems that day. He had to pass gas. It was an emergency, and he was quickly trying to figure out a way to let go without being detected. Louis was always the proper gentleman, on and off the water. It was back then when guides could carry handguns and shoot muskies next to the boat. Suddenly, he looked up and yelled, 'Look, a hawk!' With that he drew his gun, pulled the trigger on it and himself at the same time. Unfortunately, the gun didn't go off."

For some strange reason, the northern pike has a bad reputation here in the Northwoods. The number one complaint is "too many bones." Most of the bones can be cut out with a few simple waves of a sharp filleting knife. The excellent musky guide Ray Kennedy of the Minocqua chain states emphatically that the northern is the best tasting fish. He proved it once by having yours truly over for dinner and allowing our party to sample pan fried offerings of musky, walleye bass, panfish, and northern. It was sensational, and believe it or not, the most tasty was the northern. It doesn't lie flat on the taste buds; it does taste marvelous.

Louis St. Germaine also loved northern pike. After filleting them, he would put them in a meat grinder, then mix in egg, flour, salt, and other seasonings in order to make fish patties. After cooking them like hamburgers, the sizzling heat would finish off the remaining small bones. They were delicious.

Louis' wife Bertha kept a book on his guiding dates, and Louis kept another fishing book done with the meticulous care of an acountant. His special book was filled with facts and information about fishing. It contained dates, time of day, weather, wind, barometer readings, how many fish, species. It was the perfect ledger and a method that many fishing experts recommend today.

Another great Indian guide is Nelson Sheppo, also of Lac du Flambeau. Sheppo, a Pottawatamie, lives in a small gray house on Odanah Street in the city limits of Flambeau. His Indian name is *Na-Ge-Shek*, which means "Mid Day." Sheppo has been a fishing guide for 48 years and despite his age of 78 continues an active guiding career. During the rest of the time, he finds time to be an active participant in the Foster Grandparent program at the Tribal office complex. There he is known as Grandpa Sheppo. The youngsters love him.

For many years, Sheppo fished with St. Germaine, mainly out of Dillman's. He, too, mastered the raw knowledge of where the fish are at different times of the year. After moving to Lac du Flambeau in 1933 where he married a woman who had been a victim of "some bad Indian medicine," he took up guiding in 1934 when he began working for Bill Yeschek out of Yeschek's Resort on Crawling Stone Lake.

Sheppo put down his paint brush. He was working on an acrylic painting of a bear chasing a salmon in a rushing river.

"Louis was a good Indian," he said. "He was a personality. He got along with all people. He really taught me everything I know about musky fishing, like the proper time to use a black or yellow bucktail. For instance, on a clear lake like Crooked, I'd use white. And on Squirrel Lake, he recommended a natural color or a black bucktail."

Sheppo took me into his small living room-bedroom area. It showed he was a widower of some 21 years, but it was a warm and friendly room.

"Here, look at these," he said. He brought out some 12 assorted fishing poles from behind the television set. They just happened to be the best collection of fishing gear I had seen in the Northwoods. The quality was superb, all top-line equipment including some rare poles called "Panametrics."

As we talked about his 48 years as a top Indian guide, Sheppo showed me how to quickly tie a knot to a weedless No. 3 hook, which he uses for bass and walleye fishing. A couple of twists and it was done that fast.

"Thanks to Louis, I became a top fisherman. I'd be bragging if I told you that I caught 132 muskies in one season. A good secret is to use two pieces of pork rind attached to a treble hook." He showed me a jar filled with many pieces of white pork rind, three inches long. He would always use red flannel with the rind, again the same length.

"Man likes fish, and fish like the smell of man. I talked with many scuba divers who said big bass as well as muskies come over to them for a look. I think they are curious like we are."

Sheppo poured another cup of coffee.

"I remember the time Louis had a world record. It was on Sand Lake. He was using a Supreme reel and 27-pound test line. The musky hit, and he moved out so fast Louis couldn't thumb it. You knew it had to be big. It stripped his line completely. It was all the way out, and the musky broke the pole. Louis just shook his head. I've been looking for that fish ever since."

The world record for musky is 69 pounds 15 ounces, held by Art Lawton. In Wisconsin, the record is 69 pounds 11 ounces, held by Louis Spray.

"I spotted a record musky at Crooked Lake," said Sheppo. "It was as long as the oar."

Sheppo's biggest musky is 41 pounds. In the old days, a musky was only measured by weight. He also nailed a 40-pounder on Squirrel Lake, one of the most underrated lakes of the North.

"The nicest thing Louis ever said to me was that I learned 'good' from him and that I was getting to be a better fisherman than he was. He said whenever he saw me on the same lake that I was competition."

As we said good-bye outside of the small house, his hard-of-hearing dog named Grouch wandered by, lay down on the grass, and fell asleep. As I got my camera from the car, a neighbor's dog crawled into the vehicle. Sheppo laughed. The brown, shepherd-like dog got out with very little coaxing, and I drove back to Boulder Junction.

On Sunday, July 15, 1951, the Milwaukee Sentinel featured the famed Indian guide in the following story. The headline read:

**Louis St. Germaine**
### ... Muskie Guide Rates High

*Lac du Flambeau, July 14 — — Whipping up a tasty shore dinner, delivering a lecture to the Boy Scouts, compiling data for wildlife publications or guiding famous people, is all in a day's work for Wisconsin's famous Chippewa Indian guide, Louie St. Germaine.*

*Born in a wigwam on the shores of Sand Lake in 1898 at the Flambeau reservation, Louie has been guiding famous people in the waters for 31 years. He is regarded as a lucky guide and is usually booked well in advance. He has lost track of the number of muskies he has boated, but is confident it runs into the hundreds.*

*Louie can handle a fly or bait casting rod with equal skill. His specialty is fishing for muskies. His diary on muskies, which lists weather, wind, type of water fished, lures used and fish taken is regarded as one of the most complete works of its kind. His talents are by no means confined to the rod and reel.*

*In his youth Louie was a professional basketball*

*player and also a star pitcher.*

*His two charming daughters, Margie and Flossie, are
following the footsteps of their father and also are well
versed in fishing and hunting. They often accompany
him on trips.*

*"You never can tell what a muskie will do," says
Louie, "and you never can tell when one will hit. This is
why muskie fishing always will remain a top sport.*

*"One time I remember guiding a very good fisherman
for two weeks without even seeing a muskie and I fished
waters I knew had plenty of fish. Well, this man was
ready to go home when his driver happened to think of a
minor repair needed on the car. The job would take
about 20 minutes.*

*" 'What do you say, Louie?' he said. 'Shall we take just
one more swing around the point?'*

*"I quickly unloaded the rods, slipped into the boat,
and within the next five minutes we were fighting a 28-
pounder.*

*"Yes, sir, after 31 years of fishing I'll never say again
you never can tell what a muskie is going to do from the
one minute to the next."*

Louis once cautioned Billy about fishing too hard.
He had no luck one day on White Sand Lake, while
Louis and his party were hauling in musky after
musky.

"You're trying too hard," Louis said. "You're trying
to beat me. Just relax. Now don't fall asleep in the boat,
but do try and relax while fishing. It will come."

Billy said that Louis didn't fish the waters of Lac du
Flambeau exclusively. "Sometimes he'd hit the waters
of Boulder, Presque Isle, Horsehead, and Armour
lakes, to name a few."

For walleyes, Louis favored minnows and jigs.

It was a tradition with Louis that he and his guests
never wear white clothing in a boat. The fish could see
it, and it would scare them off.

Flossie said, "Fishing was a science with him. He
kept a regular book on the weather, time of day the fish

was caught, wind, and general conditions."

Flossie also recalls ice fishing with her dad. "We didn't get anything all day, and then he said, 'At 4:05 p.m. we'll get some.' At 4:05 p.m. we'd start catching. I don't know how he knew these things. Even when the mail plane went over in the afternoon he'd always say we'd catch fish soon."

### Fishing Tips from Louis No. 1

*Always sharpen hooks and to hide them from muskies and other fish paint the hooks with a flat-black paint.*

*Never wear a white shirt or any other bright color. Wear the forest greens or red. Dark is a key to avoid scaring off a fish.*

*Always keep your tackle box closed. A flopping fish in the bottom of the boat can cause severe injuries.*

*Never place your hand in the water near the side of a boat. Muskies can be vicious and will strike almost anything.*

*Stay away from white or shiny boats when stalking muskies.*

*You'll never catch fish with your lure in the boat.*

*When musky fishing, always make a figure 8 near the side of the boat. Many muskies lurk under boats.*

*A favorite musky bait: Black or brown bucktail with short strips of pork rind. Also small strips of red flannel.*

**A PAIR OF LUNKERS.** Lifelong pals, Marv Dillman (left) and Louis St. Germaine. Whether on a basketball court or fishing the waters of the Northwoods, the two always excelled.

**TRUE FRIENDS.** Baseball great Ted Williams appears to be towering over Louis, but actually Louis was standing on a lower level. The two men were great friends as well as fishing buddies.

# 5
# Baseball Great
# Ted Williams Remembers

*There is certianly something in angling . . .*
*that tends to produce a gentleness of spirit,*
*and a pure serenity of mind.*
—— The Angler
Washington Irving

The mutual respect between two greats, Ted
Williams and Louis St. Germaine, was a precious
commodity. Two super achievers in their own worlds
enjoying the sport of fishing, a common ground, on a
crystal clear lake in the Northwoods. Louis was an
excellent fastball pitcher and an all-around baseball
player. In between muskies, Ted and Louis shared a
laugh about the time in 1945 when Williams came in to
pitch for two full innings of major league baseball and
struck out one batter.

When Louis St. Germaine died, Williams reflected
on the legend of "Louis No. 1."

"I started to fish up in Wisconsin with a very
distinguished group of men and we stayed at Green
Lake. There was a Dutchman who ran it — I can't
remember his name — a very nice place. I was intro-

duced to Louis St. Germaine at that time. Got to fish with him over a period of three to four years. He was recognized then as absolutely the best musky guide in that part of the country.

"I remember distinctly one little trick he pulled on me, one which I caught him at. As you know, he used a pool cue as a fishing rod. He certainly believed in a stout rod and a strong line because in those days, as even today, they used suick bait and it required a stiff rod to handle it.

"One of his tricks with somebody who was new in the boat, when they were not looking, was to make a helluva splash right by the boat, like it had been a musky following the bait. And of course, that would shake up the angler."

Once when he was fishing with Williams and his party, the Louis St. Germaine legend grew another 10 feet. Louis guided them so well that the fishermen pulled in 43 muskies in three days. All the fish were released because, like Louis, Williams is also a great sportsman and a conservationist.

At a sports show in Milwaukee, Louis and his family stopped by the Sears booth and saw Williams. When the baseball Hall of Famer saw his old friend, Williams grabbed him and lifted him up with an affectionate hug. Williams introduced Louis to a group of executives, exclaiming, "This is the man who invented the stiff musky rod." Williams was referring to how Louis used a pool cue for fishing muskies. The stick offered the perfect stiffness with just the right amount of give.

Along the subject of inventions and ideas, Flossie remarked, "Dad gave away all his ideas. He was a very inventive person."

Margie reflected about how Louis gave away almost everything. He received a land grant from the president for his spot on White Sand Lake. He gave that away, too."

"I've got it back," said Flossie, referring to the document giving Louis the land. "Someone sent it to me before he died. There's a mouse hole in the center of it."

Margie recalled another gift from Louis. "He had this beautiful eagle feather headdress. In fact, he appeared on Chicago television with it. He gave it to each one of us. And finally he gave it to some tourist just because that person wanted it."

When news of Louis' death reached him, Williams said, "I can't tell you how bad I feel to hear the sad news, but I know he had a wonderful, full life. He probably spent more hours fishing for musky than anyone I've ever known."

*Chippewa carved ritual effigy figure*

**SPORTS STORY. The Milwaukee *Sentinel* ran this article and picture of Louis St. Germaine in its Sunday edition, July 14, 1951. The story in its entirety is reprinted on pages 52 and 53 of the text.**

# 6
# Tall Tales

*Noble by birth, yet nobler by his deeds.*
—— Tales of a Wayside Inn
Henry Wadsworth Longfellow

Jerry Loar, president of Dillman's in Lac du Flambeau, was a friend of Louis'. At the end, he also served as a pallbearer.

Marvin and Peg Dillman purchased the resort in 1935. It included a hotel, 13 buildings, and 1500 feet of frontage on White Sand Lake. They were married the first of June that year and started one of the most successful resort ventures in the United States. Incidentally, the newlyweds purchased the resort from Peg's father, Gus Peterson, a former logging foreman. He, like Louis, was an excellent fisherman.

The Dillman girls, Sauntra and Susan, married Jerry Loar and Dennis Robertson, respectively. Peg Dillman survives her husband, and the five of them continue to sell one thing: quality vacations of priceless time in the Northwoods.

Loar took us around the spacious Dillman's dining room overlooking White Sand Lake. The walls were filled with photographs of people, the famous as well as those who are not, who have been guests of Dillman's.

**THE GREAT CHIEF FROM WASHINGTON.** One of
Louis St. Germaine's favorite fishing partners was
President Dwight D. Eisenhower. Before he became
president, Ike learned firsthand that Native Americans
were being denied the right to determine whether they
could drink or not. One of his first acts in the White
House was to rectify that situation. Here he is being
made an honorary member of the Lac du Flambeau
Chippewa Indian Tribe. He was given the name of
*Gi-Ni-Wi-Ji-Jig* which means "Big Bird in the Sky."
Standing beside Ike at this July of 1965 ceremony are
George Brown, Sr. (right) and Ed "Weasel" Mitchell.
Ike's vest, headdress, and loincloth were all gifts from
the tribe.

Most held up healthy stringers of fish.

"Louis guided all sorts of people," said Loar. "He was at home with all people, all societies, and all economic groups. He could talk with the chairmen of the board of Old Line Life or McDonald's. Louis would take out a 16-year-old kid if his father requested it and teach him how to fish. He didn't have to fish with the big shots. He loved to fish. I remember the time he was out with a 16-year-old boy and he caught a 52-inch musky."

Loar laughed and said, "I remember the time we had some executives from Rogers, Arkansas. I picked them up at the airport one night, and on the way back they asked what they needed in the way of lures that they could get muskies on. We stopped at Village Hardware, and they cleaned off the lure racks. In Arkansas, people like to 'drift fish.' It's entirely different than here.

"Well, when we got back, they wanted to catch walleyes. I took them to a sand bar and caught a walleye for them. I anchored them and left. I looked out later and saw that they had pulled up and were drifting. It meant only one thing. That night it would be a hostile group because they would catch no fish.

"The next day I fixed them up with Louis. They took out two boats. By 9:30 a.m., they had a 17-pound musky and returned to shore. Out again they went. By 11 a.m., they were in again and this time with a 35-pound musky. Louis didn't say anything. He just rolled his eyes.

"After lunch, they headed out for walleyes and returned with 20-plus walleyes. Again, Louis rolled his eyes. The next morning I drove them to the airport. They said nothing. No thanks or anything. Never heard from them again. And that was a good day of fishing.

"Later, I asked Louis what happened. He said all had almost toy-like rods and reels with 8-pound test line, even for the muskies. Their casts were plops in the water. After their short casts, Louis would row the boat in circles. When the muskies got close to the boat after one got lucky, Louis would gaff it as it got close to the boat. Louis was generous, even with amateurs.

"Louis was a wonderful, proud man," Loar added. "He was very proud to be an Indian. He once said he didn't know of any disadvantages being an Indian."

Loar remembered fondly a cookout with the "Washington gang." The fishermen brought along their wives for an old-fashioned day of fishing and a famous lunch with the Indian guides. The guides for the day included Louis, Sam LaBarge, Tom Devine, Nelson Sheppo, and Roy Firpo. The site of the lunch was on a small peninsula on White Sand Lake known as Catfish Point, named after Charlie Catfish. In fact, the present cabin No. 5 at Dillman's was built by Charlie on the point and later purchased and moved by the resort.

"Sheppo was fixing coffee as hungers and thirsts quickened near the noon hour. He walked over to the lake, scooped up some water, and brought it back to the fire for coffee. One of the wives said, 'You're going to make coffee with lake water?'

"Sheppo didn't say anything. Louis said, 'Nelson, walk over to the spring and get fresh water.' Nelson walked to the other side of the peninsula and got some 'spring' water. They never knew the difference.

"Next it was Firpo's turn. He opened the cans of baked beans and placed the contents in a pan over the fire. He then opened a box of macaroni and mixed the contents with the beans. Quite puzzled by the strange concoction, one of the wives had to ask why. Firpo replied with a straight face, 'I'm giving the beans the pipe-organ effect.' "

Loar continued to reminisce.

"If we had 15 guides out for a fishing party, Louis' group would always come in with fish. He had a great trick. He would always change hats and jackets when on the water. If he left the dock with a green hat and green jacket, he would wear a red hat and a red jacket after changing in the boat. The other guides always watched where Louis went because nine out of 10 times that was the hot spot."

Peg Dillman said, "I remember Louis well. A great

fisherman and a nice man. One day I was fishing with him and made a super cast. He looked at me and said, 'Talk to me before you sign up as a guide.' "

According to Loar, Louis also fished with Earl Eisenhower (one of the president's brothers). He didn't like him, but he did like fishing with Dwight Eisenhower. He also guided Tennessee Ernie Ford as well as Gypsy Rose Lee.

His three favorite baits, Loar said, were a black bucktail, jointed Pikie minnow, and later a suick.

Louis St. Germaine and Marv Dillman were great friends and played basketball together. Dillman was 5'7" and was a great dribbler. He was a tough and determined ballplayer. Louis at 6' was quiet and aggressive. He would always grab a rebound and flip it to Marv at the other end of the court for a quick two points.

Peg added, "Marvin was one of the guys who escaped with Louis out of a coal chute to avoid an angry crowd."

The friendship between Louis and Marv began in 1928 when Dillman was going to college and working as a counselor at a boys camp in the area. Dillman also served as principal of the Lac du Flambeau school.

Peg Dillman remarked, "Louis truly was No. 1. He was a perfectionist. He would make his own lures and test his and others." She said Louis would test the lures by rowing a boat and pulling them behind. His brother Billy would swim near the lure to watch the action of the artificial bait. Peg added, "They didn't make them any better than Louis."

Dennis Robertson of Dillman's fondly recalls Louis and two fishing partners.

"They were in a long, slender guide's boat powered by one of the new sleek Evinrude motors. Attending to the motor was a guide from Colorado who was sure he was going to teach Louis how to fish. Louis sat in the bow. The fishing gent from the Rockies started the trusty Evinrude, and the 10-horse engine revved up like mad. It looked like it was at full throttle,"

Robertson mused.

"The guide panicked. He didn't know whether it was in forward or reverse and tried to spin the motor around by hand. Louis held onto the side walls as the boat's bow bounced ahead onto the dock. The motor was now in reverse, and it started to pull the boat backwards, submerging its rear end like a submarine. Louis turned slowly around and said quietly, 'You can turn off the motor now.' "

One day Louis was taking a rookie fisherman from Dillman's out for a day of musky fishing. Now this gent had never even seen a musky before. Louis, who didn't fish while he was with customers, told the man to make some casts near the bullrushes. Suddenly, the fearless angler spotted a giant musky moving toward his lure. Louis said the gent got so excited he threw his rod and reel at the musky, then simply sat down in the boat.

Louis was guiding a party on White Sand Lake, fishing for walleyes. During a lull over a sand bar, one of the men dozed off with his pole in hand. Louis reached into the cooler and pulled out a bottle of beer. Carefully, he lifted the gent's line up and tied the bottle to it, then tossed it overboard. When the bottle landed in the water, it resounded like a walleye strike, waking up the startled fisherman and triggering some quiet laughter from Louis. The first "bottle bass," no doubt.

Jerry Loar summed up his thoughts on Louis.

"He enjoyed the freedom of the North," he said. "His customers were friends and not *tourists*. Most of all, Louis was a businessman, a private contractor. People hired him for his knowledge. He believed all people should live together under one set of rules. He could move through all societies and ethnic backgrounds without a hitch.

"I think, too, that Louis practiced good conservation because of the basic economics of it. People would spend money to catch fish. And taking too many fish out of the lakes would hurt his business. He didn't like commercialization. He loved the sport. Take what you need and nothing more was what he promoted. Fish to him were worth much more swimming around. He appreciated the natural resources here."

Shirley Baucaro of Maywood Lodge in Lac du Flambeau remembers the time Louis St. Germaine came into her bar during a break in the fishing action. She was busy cleaning the bar area and her hair was in curlers.

In a quiet manner, Louis looked at her and said, "I wouldn't come in here with shaving cream on my face."

Shirley, who along with her husband Bob donates many long hours to the town fire and ambulance service, added that whenever Louis made a comment it was always in a friendly manner.

"I don't think he had an unkind bone in his body," she concluded.

*Chippewa Ceremonial Drum and smaller water drum*

**ENJOYING A LITTLE COMRADERIE.** Ted Williams and Louis St. Germaine relax on shore, sharing a little lunch and perhaps a few good stories about the ones that got away. From the looks on their faces, Williams is telling Louis a story, and Louis is getting ready to burst out laughing at the punchline. Both men loved a good yarn, and both were known to play practical jokes on each other as well as other unsuspecting fishermen. One of Louis' favorite tricks was to slap the water near the boat when his customer began to doze off in the warm summer sun, startling whoever the recipient of his humor might be into thinking a big musky had just jumped nearby.

# 7
# Catching Up With A Legend

*There were things which he stretched,*
*but mainly he told the truth.*
—— The Adventures of Huckleberry Finn
Mark Twain

Louis always loved stories.

One day, as Louis told it, he and his mother were sitting on the porch of their home. All was silent except for the sound of a pack of wolves who were chasing a deer toward the lake. His mother said he should go get the deer because "we need meat." Louis grabbed the paddles and a gun and headed out in a canoe. Once out in the lake and near the deer, Louis reached for the gun but grabbed the canoe paddles instead. It was too late. He then grabbed the tail of the deer and tied it to the front of the canoe. Near shore, the deer flipped the canoe.

The following year when Louis was fishing for wall-eyes on the shore he saw a strange sight on the other side of the lake. He wandered over and saw a scene that was hard to believe. It was the same deer towing the canoe. Only this time, there were two fawns in the canoe.

Louis was also fond of telling the tale about his pet bass. Each day it seemed Louis would entice the bass on the shore. Each day it would stay a little longer out of the water. After a year, the bass could stay out of the water all day and even follow him to town. One day Louis walked to town. There was no bass with him. "What happened?" a friend asked him. Louis said that his bass was on the pier one day and fell into the water where he drowned.

Perhaps the true meaning of why Louis never left the reservation was a page one story on December 14, 1964 in the Chicago *Tribune*. It was written by Pulitzer Prize winner Tom Fitzpatrick. The story was accented by a precede:

*There are nearly 900 members of the Chippewa Indian tribe living on the Lac du Flambeau reservation in Northern Wisconsin. But despite the beauty of their surroundings, the tribe members face a fight for existence during the winter months. They have little food and there are no jobs they can get to earn money . . .*

*Lac du Flambeau, Wis., Dec 13 — He's become a legend in his own lifetime, but he's also a symbol of the Chippewa tribesman's dilemma.*

*Louis St. Germaine is 66 years old and there isn't a man in Vilas county who couldn't point him out on the street or tell a stranger where he lives.*

*They speak of him in hushed tones as "Big Louis" or "Louis No. 1" because of his abilities as an athlete, fisherman, hunter and guide. He's one of the best the modern Chippewas have ever seen.*

*In St. Germaine's youth he was such an outstanding basketball player that he once made a tour with the original Celtics. He was a semi-pro baseball pitcher with a fast ball that is still recalled by old-timers.*

*But despite these athletic abilities and an acute intelligence, St. Germaine never wanted to leave the area where he had been born. There's a grip that the reser-*

vation gains on each one of its natives.

Some call it an invisible prison because there is no way to gain economic success while here, and no way to be happy anywhere else.

"I took a job at Elgin high school for 10 years," St. Germaine said, "but I had a clause in my contract so that I could leave in May to come back for fishing and not return until November.

"I've been a guide for 40 years now," said this man who was a machine gun instructor during World War I, "and I've had some thrills during my lifetime."

When pressed for details, he immediately recalled the day that he had served as a guide for Ted Williams, the baseball player.

"I remember, once, when I was young," he said, "that I went on tour with an Indian basketball team. We were good but the only time people showed interest was during the halftime when we came out to do a pow-wow dance.

"Then, as we got further west, the crowds began getting smaller. They had their own Indians out there. But we were very big in the East."

St Germaine smiled wryly before continuing.

"Sure, I suppose I thought about moving to the city, sometimes," he said, "but the city was never a place for me. I could never feel comfortable. I just want to be in the woods I guess."

He was asked about John St. Germaine, who in 1941 at the age of 21, saved the lives of three Chicago politicians when their boat tipped over on Crawling Stone Lake near here.

"Sure I remember him," said St. Germaine. "He was a distant cousin. Those three men he saved put up the money to send him through the University of Wisconsin. I believe he's still a pharmacist in Madison."

But the manner St. Germaine related this story made it evident that any tribe member who leaves the reservation and doesn't return is not really remembered by anyone.

A man who leaves has chosen a different world, one that is thousands of years removed from the reservation where many things are still done as in the days of the

*French voyageurs.*

*There was nothing more to say. St. Germaine accompanied his visitor to the door.*

*"Before you leave," he said, "go down to the Flame, that's a tavern in the center of town. Take a look at the musky hanging on the walls. Find the two biggest fish. Those are mine."*

*St. Germaine spoke the truth.*

*There were more than 50 fish mounted on the walls. Each had a plaque which told its size, the man who caught the fish and the guide.*

*Under the two largest musky in the dimly lit room was appended the name: Louis St. Germaine.*

The headline on the jump page in the *Tribune* told it like it was:

## Dilemma of Indians: Success or Happiness

The reporter who wrote the piece, Tom Fitzpatrick, returned to the big city and pursued a troubled newspaper career. He is a brilliant writer. The last I heard of Fitz, who won the Pulitzer for the days of rage during the Democratic National Convention in Chicago in 1968, was that he was writing "in Arizona." A lonely jogger on the Chicago lakefront, one of Fitz's most haunting lines in his column in the Chicago *Sun Times* was, ". . . I continue to run, but sometimes I wonder where I'm running to . . ."

*Chippewa Beadwork*

*Louis No. 1*

**FISHING BUDDIES.** Northwoods fishing guide Harvey Bagley (right) poses with a friend, Gen. Dwight D. Eisenhower, during a lunch break while fishing near Boulder Junction, Wisconsin. A friend of Louis St. Germaine, Bagley said, "Louis was a great one. They threw away the mold after he was born."

**A GOOD FRIEND.** Maylin Ruff owner and operator of Ruff's Amour Lake Resort, was a good friend of Louis St. Germaine. Ruff, as everyone calls him, was asked to compare Louis with Porter Dean, and Ruff replied, "Don't ask me that."

# 8

# Maylin Ruff Remembers

*Life in the wilderness can be a continual contemplation
and communion with God and Spirit of those values
echoing within us all, values born of timelessness, mys-
tery, the great silences, and an ancient way of life.*
—— Reflections from the North Country
Sigurd F. Olson

*Memory: what wonders it performs in preserving and
storing up things.*
—— Plutarch

I first heard about Maylin Ruff from fishing guide
Tommy Newcomb. "He knew Louis well," he said.

It was a crisp fall day as I headed through the maze of
leaves on County Trunk Highway B on the way to
Presque Isle, known as the "Walleye Capital of the
World." It was beautiful. The weather was turning
violent and swirls of leaves colored the drive. I turned
left on Crab Lake Road in search of Maylin and Kathy
Ruff's Armour Lake Resort on Big Horsehead and
Armour Lakes. A yellow caution sign on the road read:

"Rough Road Ahead." There was a line slashed through the word *rough* and the name *Ruff* inked in on top of it.

The waves were lashing the shore of Armour Lake as I headed for the office. Kathy let me in. Maylin was at his desk writing some checks.

"Welcome," he said, extending a rugged hand.

Ruff had been a resort owner for 19 years, having moved north from Racine, Wisconsin nearly two decades earlier. We had already discussed the purpose of my visit, so he got right to the point.

"So you want to know about Louis," he said. Then quickly, he added, "He was a real good man. I would trust him with anything. The guests here loved him. We would have to go to Lac du Flambeau and pick him up. He couldn't drive. He fished here at least two or three times a week."

"What did Louis use for bait for his walleyes?" I asked.

"Minnows, female minnows. When someone asked him why he caught so many walleyes, he'd always say, 'Female minnows.' Of course, you couldn't tell. But Louis would feel around in the minnow bucket until he'd say, 'Got one,' and proceed to place a 'female' minnow on his hook.

"Louis used a lot of psychology in his fishing. He knew a good story and a good time were sometimes more important than catching fish. He knew how to take care of people and please them.

"Louis loved to tell stories. One comes to mind. He said he was out fishing with a Jewish woman and her husband. They owned a great big department store in Chicago. They were wealthy, and she was good looking. She was sitting in the front end of the boat, and he was rowing around finding spots to fish. She had on a halter and a little triangular thing on her bottom area. She said to Louis, 'Do you mind if I take off my halter?' Louis said the only halter he ever heard of was on a horse, so he said go ahead. She took off her halter, and Louis rowed like a mad bat around the lake."

Kathy, Maylin's wife of 34 years, poured us another cup of coffee, and he went on.

"Louis always liked to tell the story of fishing with Bing Crosby. He took Bing walleye fishing one day. Everytime he would get a hit, Bing would yank the hook out of the walleye's mouth. Now everyone knows you have to let the walleye take the bait, then set the hook. Again, Bing let one get away. Finally, Louis told him, 'Bing, when you get a bite, sing one chorus of *Auld Lang Syne.*'

"Louis is the main reason Indians can drink today."

That was startling news, but upon researching the subject, I found that since 1834 federal law has specifically prohibited the introdcution of liquor into an Indian reservation and that possession of liquor in Indian country has been a crime since 1918. A 1953 statute allows these laws to be conditionally suspended on any reservation by an enactment of the governing tribe. In other words, it was against the law for Indians to drink until the early '50s.

Ruff explained his claim. "Before Louis guided (then Gen. Dwight D.) Eisenhower, before he was ever anything, it was Ike who first noticed the problem. Now Ike liked to drink a bit, as did Louis. Ike would walk into a tavern and get a six-pack of beer and take it out to the car. Louis would be in the car. He couldn't go into the tavern, and that really bothered Ike. Louis would be in the car drinking by himself, while Ike and his cronies would be in the tavern drinking. Ike said at one time, and this was years ago, that if he ever got to be anything, he would see to it that the Indians could drink just as the whites could. That was one of the first things he ever did when he got to be president."

In July of 1965, a ceremony was conducted in Lac du Flambeau that Ike always maintained was the highlight of his visits to the North, according to author Joyce Laabs, a personal friend of Ike and Mamie. That summer Ike became an honorary member of the Lac du Flambeau Chippewa Indian Tribe.

Alex Bobidosh was tribal chairman at the time and

also a colorful figure, Laabs wrote in her fascinating book, *Northwoods Nostalgia*. Alex, like Louis, played football at the Indian college, Carlisle Institute. He also traveled to California to build a birch bark house that was to become part of the Frontier Village at Disneyland.

The Chippewa community selected a name for Ike. It was *Gi-Ni-Wi-Ji-Jig*, which means, "Big Bird in the Sky." On the big day, all roads to Lac du Flambeau were bumper-to-bumper. It was a most impressive ceremony. Ike was given a Chippewa headdress: a single feather held by a roach of porcupine hair. Stylized beadwork made up the headband, with the name Ike in beads on the front part of the band. Alex presented him with beaded moccasins, and members of the tribe gave him a jacket and loincloth. Mamie, Mrs. Eisenhower, was given a beautiful beaded purse.

President Eisenhower died on March 29, 1969. He will long be remembered by all Indians, but especially by the Chippewa, for restoring one more basic freedom to them: the right to choose whether they want to drink or not.

Ruff got back to his friend Louis St. Germaine. "You asked me earlier what I really thought of him. I always recalled his honesty and integrity.

"It was November, and we were closed. I was out getting wood. Louis came up with two of his compadres. They were all pretty well gassed. They weren't out fishing or nothing. They were just out riding around, drinking. Louis came to the door to see if the bar was open. Kathy opened it for them. They had a few drinks, and Louis called Kathy into the hallway. He said, 'Here, Kathy, save this for me.' He had a big roll of bills. It was a lot money. Louis said he just wanted to have her keep the money which he got by just cashing some checks. His friends knew he had the money. He wanted to make sure he wasn't rolled. Kathy wanted to give him a receipt, but Louis said he trusted her."

Kathy found an old weathered photograph of an aging Louis with two customers he brought to Armour

Lake from Lac du Flambeau. It was a typical vacation snapshot. The three were herded against the left side of the picture, while the rest of the lens captured air. But Louis and the man and woman were holding a nice stringer of walleyes.

"Well, they came back the next day, thinking it was so easy to catch walleyes like with Louis the day before. They were out all day and caught nothing. They even hit the same spots and used 'female' minnows. Nothing. It got to be 10 p.m., and we got a call from concerned relatives in Lac du Flambeau as to the whereabouts of the fishermen. They finally came in. No fish. Louis was a master. He sensed where the fish were."

Ruff laughed and added, "Everytime he'd come here, it was a show. He'd walk over to Big Horsehead Lake and pretend he was sniffing the air, perhaps, for fish smells. Then he'd walk over to Armour Lake and sniff the air again. His customers would always watch intently. Then in dramatic fashion, he'd always pick a lake to fish with such finality."

Kathy said that anytime Louis was fishing, the resort guests would hide behind trees with "spy-glasses" and watch him fish the shoreline and brush piles for walleyes. When Louis and his fishing customers would come ashore for a resort lunch, guests would always pop down to his boat to check his rigs and try to pick up his fishing techniques.

"How would you compare Porter Dean and Louis?" I asked.

Ruff shook his head and looked away for a second. "Don't ask me that question."

I dropped the subject and let him go on.

"Louis liked to have a drink now and then. When he'd come into the resort, he'd always say, 'Need a coupla seat cushions.' That was a signal. I'd always walk with him down to the bar and get him a brandy and a beer wash. That was it. he was never drunk while guiding anyone. He felt the time to relax was after a successful day on the water. He never ever had too much while taking someone out. That was the difference between Louis and many of the Indian guides."

Ruff related how Louis would bring his customers into the resort and they would sing while Ruff played the piano. I asked if Louis could sing, and Maylin replied, "Couldn't sing worth a damn!"

Ruff is an ex-marine, a drill instructor with the Corps in San Diego during World War II. After sharing a couple of war stories about my encounters with DI's, Ruff recalled some tales.

"It was during war time, and we had to have fun with the recruits, to toughen them up. We'd come back a little looped some nights and get the recruits up and march them into the bay up to their necks. We'd laugh. When I got home after the war, I always thought some son-of-a-bitch would come and look me up and get me. But we toughened them up. I was mean, but that was my job."

Ruff dropped the subject and returned to his friend Louis St. Germaine.

"There's a walleye hole near cabin 3 on Big Horsehead. Louis would always row over it before starting his motor. Catch two or three walleyes for his customers and then head out. Do it everytime. Uncanny! I put a pier out near the hole one day, and Louis said I could improve the fishing quality by getting a salt block, like the ones you put out for deer. Wrap it, he said, in three sets of burlap sacks. And put it near the end of the pier. It would disintegrate and attract fish. He said I will have the finest fishing hole in the lake. And today because of that fact, it is still the finest fishing spot in the lake."

We shared a couple of wild musky stories and discussed how really dangerous they are. The muskies are the "Jaws" stories of the Northwoods. People get bitten — attacked — often requiring many stitches to close big mouth wounds. The musky attack stories rarely leave the Northwoods, lest the tourists get frightened, and the "Escape to Wisconsin" theme might be replaced by "Escape to the safety of your nearby Holiday Inn pool in Oak Brook, Illinois."

But a musky is as great a sport fish as it is vicious. I know one Wisconsin Department of Natural Resources fishery biologist who sustained a 17-stitch gash to his foot, attacked by a musky as he was pulling in a fish net. One of the signs of summer at the Howard Young Medical Center in Woodruff, Wis., is when a nurse yells, "Where are we doing fishing hooks today?"

Ruff recalled when one of his guests, a young school teacher, watched as her boyfriend pulled in a musky off the pier. She got excited and ran down to the pier, thrilled at the sight of seeing a savage musky. She thought it would be easy to do the same thing and picked up a musky rod with its "Daredevil" lure attached. She thrust out a mighty cast. Unfortunately, she didn't catch a musky but did catch her boyfriend's nose with the lure. It was a deep "hook." You couldn't push it through. The Ruffs rushed him to the Catholic hospital in Wakefield, Michigan. A nun walked by this gent in the hospital. She stopped, walked past again, then came back again. She looked at him and laughed, seeing this giant lure hanging from his nose. "It's a good thing you weren't fishing with worms," she said.

"I recalled one day" Ruff said, "when Louis received a big box from Ted Williams. He was proud of that. It was an assortment of some 15 reels that Ted sent him to test for Sears. It was filled with lures. They were great friends. One of the old stories was that if you saw a yellow Cadillac parked alongside the side of the road at 4 a.m., that was Ted and Louis sleeping one off. They were great friends."

Ruff scratched his head and added, "The one day I remember most was when he arrived at Armour Lake Resort early one morning with two Chicagoans for breakfast. They seemed real nervous, so I asked him why. He told me that he had another guiding job that same day at noon back at the Flame in Lac du Flambeau, so he was anxious to get out there and get his fishermen a quick limit of walleyes.

"Louis came off the water about 10:30 a.m. all shook

up! When asked what was the matter, he replied that he had taken 14 walleyes and had actually caught the 15th one when while handing the fish to the customer to put on a stringer the fellow dropped all 15 walleyes to the bottom of the lake.

"After a quick trip to Chet's for more minnows, the three were fishing again. He left the resort that day at 12:30 with 15 more walleyes and two satisfied customers, heading for the Flame in Flambeau to catch his second guiding job of the day."

The Ruffs showed me the bar where Louis and his satisfied customers quaffed a brew or two. It looked like a fun place as I imagined Louis No. 1 standing there, sharing a tale or three with his friends.

Outside, they said good-bye as I headed back to "Ruff Road Ahead." Dark gray clouds and a snappy wind were heavy in the late-morning sky. It was the first real touch of cold. The wind would knock out trapped pockets of warm summer air in the Northern Highland State Forest, officially ending the warm season. A year earlier eight inches of snow socked the Northwoods. I wondered what Louis St. Germaine would have been doing on a day like this.

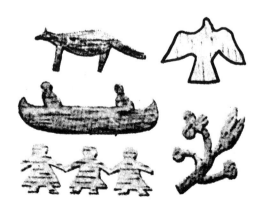

*Chippewa Birch Bark Cutout Figures*

**SUPER GUIDE.** Fishing guide Harvey Bagley of Boulder Junction was one of the super guides of the Northwoods to be associated with Louis St. Germaine. Here Bagley and customer Willard Cox display a nice stringer of fish. According to musky guide Bill Gleason, Bagley was like Louis No. 1 — in a class by himself.

**UNSURPASSED AMONG MEN. Louis St. Germaine as he appeared in later life. One writer wrote how Louis was a great man among modern Chippewas. It's this writer's opinion that he was a great man for all men in all times. Maybe he wasn't a great political leader who left an indelible mark on history, but he was a great man all the same when measured by the size of his spirit.**

# 9
# Unsurpassed Among Men

*Make me ever ready to come to you,*
*With clean hands,*
*and straight eyes,*
*So that*
*When life fades as the fading sunset,*
*My spirit may come to you,*
*Without shame.*
—— Chippewa Prayer
Tom Whitecloud II

*We can never have enough of that*
*Which we really do not want.*
—— Eric Hoffer

*Life is an unanswered question,*
*but let's believe in the dignity*
*and importance of the question.*
—— Tennessee Williams

St. Valentine's Day, February 14, 1983

Louis was dying. His body was riddled with cancer.

There was much pain, but you wouldn't know it from his lips. There was nothing but silence. Only his eyes hinted at the ferocity of the agony behind them.

Flossie entered his hospital room.

"Out of the blue," Flossie said to me later, "he mentioned the word charcoal. 'Flossie, look into charcoal.' He added that it was not a lump of charcoal, but that it was in a different form."

Louis went silent again. Flossie talked. Again, Louis mentioned the word charcoal and that something was "very, very wrong."

It was getting late, and Flossie left the hospital and returned home about 6 p.m.

When she returned home that evening, her husband Willis said the hospital had called and said something had happened to her teenage grandson David. Apparently, he had taken a couple of swallows of hard whiskey on a dare from his friends. He had passed out and was then in the emergency room of the Howard Young Medical Center in Woodruff, Wis., located just east of Lac du Flambeau.

Her grandson was a model youth. "He was always good and never got into trouble," Flossie said, her eyes fixed on the new-falling snow outside.

Flossie drove her white Thunderbird east on State Highway 70 to the hospital, then hurried into the emergency room. She was familiar with the room as she had been there many times as a health and welfare counselor. The doctor was working on David. He was coming around. A smile crossed her worried face as David recognized her. He was out of danger.

While standing with her back against a wall, she happened to look into a nearby wastebasket. There was an empty container of liquid charcoal in the basket. The charcoal had been used to absorb the whiskey in David's stomach.

Flossie paused a moment, taking a sip of hot instant coffee. "It was then that a chill went up my spine. I remembered my father's words about charcoal."

Margie then repeated the story about her Uncle

Joe's death. I enter it here again because of the connection with the charcoal episode.

"I remember one night. It was raining heavy. I was home. It was a terrible rain. Late that night, I heard three knocks on the back door. I opened the door and nobody was there. Again, three more knocks. Again, nobody there. Knocks again. My aunt went to the door. Nobody there. The next day I went to school. And they said, 'Did you hear your Uncle Joe died?' He was drowned. Later, they were dragging the lake, but they couldn't find these people. (Uncle Joe and the two fishermen with him.) They found one but couldn't find the other two.

"And older Indian came to see my dad and told him to go see the medicine man and bring some tobacco. Lay the tobacco down and just wait. He told my dad exactly where the one man would be. He would be clutching an oar, standing upright at the bottom of the lake. And then he told my dad exactly where my Uncle Joe was."

Few understand what magnet draws the Indian back to his reservation. Louis always came back. Indians today are damned by many as lazy; they have no ambition, some say. The folly of that thinking stems from ignorance. Perhaps Charles Alexander Eastman in his book *The Soul of the Indian* unearthed the roots of the ignorance of whites toward the Indian.

". . . It was not, then, wholly from ignorance or improvidence that he failed to establish permanent towns and to develop material civilization. To the untutored sage, the concentration of population was the prolific mother of all evils, moral no less than physical. He argued that food is good, while surfeit kills; that love is good, but lust destroys; and not less dreaded than the pestilence following upon crowded and unsanitary dwellings was the loss of spiritual power inseparable from too close contact with one's fellow men. All who have lived much out of doors know there is a magnetic and nervous force that accumulates in solitude and that is quickly dissipated by life in a crowd; and even his enemies have recognized the fact that for a certain innate power and self-poise, wholly independent of circumstance, the American Indian is unsurpassed among men."

I offer this as an epitaph for the man of this work.

*Have you suffered, starved or triumphed,*
*   groveled down, yet grasped at glory,*
*Grown bigger in the bigness of the whole?*
*"Done things" just for the doing,*
*   letting babblers tell the story,*
*Seeing through the nice veneer the naked soul?*
*Have you seen God in His splendors,*
*   heard the text that nature renders?*
*(You'll never hear it in the family pew.)*
*The simple things, the true things,*
*   the silent men who do things - -*
*     Then listen to the Wild - -*
*       it's calling you.*

—— Robert Service
The Call of the Wild

Robert Service never met Louis St. Germaine, but he knew him. They were kin in the silent wilds. When Service penned those memorable lines, he was truly writing about the silent one — Louis St. Germaine, Louis No. 1.

*Chippewa Owl Effigy*

*Louis No. 1*

**LAC DU FLAMBEAU BY AIR.** This view from high above shows some of the lakes around Lac du Flambeau.

**SHORE LUNCH.** Enjoying a fabled shore lunch in the Northwoods during a break in the fishing action are Gen. Dwight D. Eisenhower and his brothers. Also enjoying the feast are Howard Young, Roy Aken, Mickey Lambert, and Harvey Bagley, another great fishing guide. The shore lunch used to be one of the highlights of a fishing trip to the Northwoods. The Eisenhowers were frequent visitors to Wisconsin before Ike became president in 1953. Ike was very popular among the guides, and the Chippewas especially cared for him. The tribe honored Eisenhower by making him an honorary member of the Chippewa Nation.

**JUST BROWSING. Dwight D. Eisenhower (right) and his brother Arthur browse around the shoreline of a Northwoods lake looking for a lunker bass or two. Most of the guides of the Northwoods loved to fish with Ike and called him one of their own.**

**FAMOUS ACTRESS ENJOYING FAVORITE PASTTIME.** Actress Elizabeth Taylor was only 15 when this photograph of her was taken. Miss Taylor is an accomplished bass fisherman. Her favorite bait was a Stanley weedless with a pork chunk. While in the Northwoods, the young Miss Taylor wrote a children's book entitled, *Nibbles and Me*. The book featured the tale of her exploits with a friendly chipmunk. It also featured many sketches by the author.

BAREFOOT FISHING GUIDE. Whenever the
Wisconsin Department of Natural Resources
needed some promo shots, they'd always call on
the late Porter "Barefoot" Dean of Boulder
Junction. He was a master at spinning fishing
fables, especially at one of his delicious shore
lunches. In all the years I knew him, I could never
tell when he was putting me on.

**HAPPY CUSTOMER. When guide Jim Peck (right) talked about fishing, people listened. Jim and a happy customer show off a day's catch.**

**CELEBRATION.** Members of the Lac du Flambeau Chippewa tribe pose in their native dress for a 4th of July celebration.

**QUIET MAIN STREET.** Lac du Flambeau's main street as it looked in the 1920s. Just another peaceful day in the Northwoods.

AT THE TURN OF THE CENTURY. Lac du Flambeau was a lumber town of sorts at the turn of the century as witnessed by this photograph taken around 1905. Note the logging chute in the foreground and the logs floating in the water. Also note the large house in the center. That is the Gauthier Hotel.

# Appendix A

*Excerpt from "The Soul of the Indian" by Charles Alexander Eastman.*

". . . the Red Man divided mind into two parts — the spiritual mind and the physical mind. The first is pure spirit, concerned only with the essence of things, and it was this he sought to strengthen by spiritual prayer, during which the body is subdued by fasting and hardship. In this type of prayer there was no beseeching of favor or help. All matters of personal or selfish concern, as success in hunting or warfare, relief from sickness, or the sparing of a beloved life, were definitely relegated to the plane of the lower or material mind, and all ceremonies, or incantation designed to secure a benefit or to avert danger, were recognized as emanating from the physical self . . ."

*Chippewa Hawk Effigy*

# Appendix B

*Chief Sealth of the Duwanish Tribe from Washington State sent this letter to Pres. Franklin Pierce in 1855.*

*The Great Chief in Washington sends word that he wishes to buy our land. How can you buy or sell the warmth of the land? The idea is strange to us. Yet we do not own the freshness of the air or the sparkle of the water. How can you buy them from us? Every part of this earth is sacred to my people. Every shiny pine needle, every shady shore, every mist in the dark woods, every clearing and humming insect is holy in the memory of my people.*

*We know that the white man does not understand our ways. One portion of the land is the same to him as the next, for he is a stranger who comes in the night and takes from the land whatever he needs. The earth is not his brother but his enemy, and when he has conquered it he moves on. He leaves his fathers' graves, and his children's birthright is forgotten.*

*There is no quiet place in the white man's cities. No place to hear the leaves of spring or the rustle of insect wings. But perhaps because I am a savage and do not understand, the clatter only seems to insult the ears. And what is there to life if a man cannot hear the lovely cry of the whippoorwill or the argument of the frog around the pond at night?*

*The whites too shall pass, perhaps sooner than other tribes. Continue to contaminate your own bed and you will one night suffocate in your own waste.*

*When the buffalo are all slaughtered, the wild horses all tamed, the secret corners of the forest heavy with the scent of many men, and the view of the ripe hills blotted by talking wires, where is the thicket? Gone. Where is the eagle? Gone. And what will it be to say good-bye to the swift and the hunt? It will be the end of living and the beginning of survival.*

# Appendix C

*A prayer.*

Great Spirit, let us give thanks for food and shelter
    during the long moons of our lives.
For the rain and sun that gave light, love and beauty to
    us your children.
For your guidance and protection on the many trails in
    our lifetime.
Great Chief, grant these graduates the wisdom of our
    elders, the strength and endurance of our Mother,
    the earth.
May the sunshine of understanding be planted in their
    hearts for many sleeps, for many moons and many
    winters.
Great Spirit, may their moccasin trails through life be
    draped with peace and the rainbow always touch
    their shoulders.
Amen.

*Dorothy Poupart*

# Appendix D

*Thoughts from Chapter 18 of Ivan Clyde Lake's 1931 book, "Minocqua". The book was reprinted in 1974 by Four Winds Publishing Co., of Minocqua, Wisconsin.*

Sixteen miles from Minocqua the Chippewa Indians — the Ojibwas of Longfellow's *Hiawatha* — occupy the Flambeau Reservation of 68,814 acres in parts of Vilas, Iron and Oneida counties.

Always, according to one interpreter, the Chippewa has been a friend of the white man. Certainly he often met with his pale-skinned brother in the days when the Caucasian was coming into the Northland to destroy his forests and kill his game and deplete his lakes.

Submersion by the white man has not yet occurred to the Indian of the North Country; copper skins, paled by Caucasian admixture, were not so generally known as now. The Red Man was gloriously Indian, gloriously pagan, and comparatively free from the ennervations of modern civilization.

The native Flambeauans now dress in our attire, drive our discarded Fords, eat our canned goods; but at heart they are markedly racial. Even among the half-breeds there is an atavism that holds them to Indian ways, albeit one student of the Red Man declares that mixed bloods tend to show an initiative unknown to the tawny purebreds that causes them to break away from Reservation life.

With the advent of the white man's civilization, many of the ancient Indian customs gradually disappeared. Custom marriage, for example, is no longer the fashion on the Reservation, although we have seen it performed in other parts of the Northland, and its legality is recognized the same as nuptials solemnized by the Christian community.

An interpreter once told us: "In the days of custom marriages we never heard of divorces. Now we are no different from the white man. We marry and separate the same as he.

"The Indian was never a polygamist. He had one wife; that was enough; he was content with her. There was no adultery. If a man sinned he was severely punished. He was placed on a high scaffold and left to dry until the crows ate him, or he was staked to the ground and there left."

The Rev. G. E. E. Linquist, student of the North American Indian, remarked to us apropos of this: "Monogamy was pronounced among the Indians. Sometimes the chiefs had more than one wife, but the others were strict monogamists. Girls were protected. But the transition has somewhat wrought havoc. The moral hazards have been great and the Indian, weaker, has yielded to the white man's ways."

Christianity, represented by the Roman Cahtolic Church and a Presbyterian, has attempted to influence the native Flambeauans to a conformity with the white man's religious beliefs. Part of the population, however, still remains pagan; it lives and dies in the superstitions and fears of its forbears.

The Indian was not originally a monotheist. Like all primitive peoples he believed in many gods. Characteristiclly of this were the Sioux. The name for their gods or Great Spirits, was Wau-Kan. Wau-Kan, the same as manito, represented the magic or supernatural forces in Nature. But when the Indian was Christianized the name for his gods was added to and became Wau-Kan-tanka, which might be translated "Heavenly Father," and would indicate somewhat the conception of one God which belongs to Christian theology.

The Indian has attained to a certain culture, to a marked expression of beauty that belongs indigenously to him. He is a poet and an artist. His legends have the high imagination of poetry in them. His pottery, his blanket-weaving, his beadwork, evince undeniable artistic accomplishments. He has been an eloquent orator — for Red Jacket, Seneca, Tecumseh, and other sachems, truly possessed silver tongues.

But what of Mr. Lo, the poor Indian of today? Is his a "vanishing race?" The Rev. Mr. Linquist does not believe so. He declared to us:

"There is an increase, rather than a decrease, in the Indian population, but the increase is much more noticeable among the mixed bloods. There is considerable intermarriage. This is not only between different tribes but between the whites and reds. There is a process of assimilation working out.

"There is a noticeable urban-ward movement of the Indians as well as our white man. I mean that Indians are leaving the Reservations for the cities and there obtaining work. There are thousands of Indians employed in the city of Detroit, and the same is true in Milwaukee, in Sioux City, and in other cities. This would indicate that the modern Indian is becoming self-reliant and independent.

"The policy of the government is not to crush the Indians, nor to extinguish tribal life. Its purpose is to conserve the best in the Red Man's past: his self-respect, generosity, hospitality, loyalty, honesty, friendliness. The solution of the 'Indian problem,' I think, is an assimilation. The Indian must be educated; there must be an intelligent industrial program for him; and he must be taught conservation of his health; and he must have the influence of Christian civilization."

# Appendix E

*"The Chippewa People of Lake Superior" is an excerpt from the marvelous book "Around the Shores of Lake Superior: A Guide to Historic Sites" by Margaret Beattie Bogue and Virginia A. Palmer, published by the University of Wisconsin Sea Grant College Program. It is copyrighted 1979 by the University of Wisconsin Board of Regents.*

Of all the Indian people of Lake Superior, the Chippewa have figured most prominently in the recorded history of the region. Three names — Chippewa, Ojibway and Ojibwa — are used to refer to the same tribe, which dates from the 17th century in the Lake Superior area. The two names most frequently used today are Chippewa, thought to be an English corruption of Ojibwa; and Ojibwa which means to "roast until puckered," referring to puckered moccasin seams. The American Bureau of Ethnology adopted the designation Chippewa early in the century, reflecting the wishes of many tribal members. Today younger tribal members prefer the term Ojibwa, now used most exclusively in Canada. Both Chippewa and Ojibwa are used in the United States.

According to anthropologists, the Chippewa Indians were part of a very large migration of Indians from the East into the Sault Ste. Marie-Mackinac area of the 17th century. From there, the Chippewas pressed west around the shores of Lake Superior, into northern Minnesota, North Dakota and southern Manitoba. Extremely courageous and successful warriors, the Chippewa had little trouble expanding their territory in the Lake Superior-Lake Huron area. They managed to drive the Sioux across the Mississippi and beyond, until Chippewa territory spread as far west as the headwaters of the Red River, located in what is now western Minnesota and North Dakota. They were in constant conflict with the Fox tribe and eventually drove that tribe out of northern Wisconsin with the help of the French.

With the French, however, the Chippewa were uniformly friendly. They engaged in fur trade with the French and later after the fall of New France, with the British and Americans. Until the close of the War of 1812, they resisted the westward tide of white settlement and provided a real challenge to Catholic and Protestant missionaries who found their native religion deeply ingrained. The Medewiwin, a tribal medicine society, exerted much influence and for many decades dictated the migrations of the tribe.

Under pressure from American and Canadian settlers, the Chippewa gradually gave up their native hunting grounds during the 19th century. By treaties, the Canadian and American governments gathered them together on reservations. With the exception of two small bands that moved west, the Chippewa were settled in the Superior-Huron area by the U. S. government.

Romanticized memories of Chippewa life in past centuries live on in the minds of many Americans who have read Henry Wadsworth Longfellow's famous poem, "Song of Hiawatha." The character Hiawatha is a Victorian version of the legendary Chippewa hero, Nanabazhoo. Part of the Chippewa cultural legacy lives on in legends collected from 1903-1905 by William Jones and published by the American Ethnological Society. The legends make delightful reading, particularly relating to Nanabazhoo. Historian Grace Lee Nute characterized him as the "combined Messiah, Puck, Prometheus and Loki of the Chippewa." He was their aid and protector, who brought them fire and discovered tobacco. He is the Sleeping Giant of Thunder Bay.

Chippewa legends also offer delightful explanations

for the shape of land forms, the origin and physical appearance of the animals of the area and the behavior of the weather and the lake. Travelers will hear these legnds from time to time as they tour around the lake shore. One such Chippewa legend attributes the origin of Lake Superior whitefish to a domestic tragedy. An Indian husband found his wife guilty of infidelity and murdered her. Her spirit returned to haunt her two children who ran away to escape it. She chased them to the St. Mary's River, where a crane gathered up all three to ferry them over the river. During the crossing, the mother fell into the rapids where she was transformed into the whitefish, a very important fish to the Indians of the Sault.

Another example of Chippewa culture can be found along the shores of Lake Superior — picture writing or pictographs. Some of the drawings include moose, deer, Indian warriors, home and canoes. . . . Henry Schoolcraft, the famous U. S. Indian agent at Sault Ste. Marie who recorded so much about the ways of the Chippewa life for posterity, interpreted a few of these Indian paintings but the meaning of many others is lost. . .

All (of the nine Chippewa Indian Reservations scattered around the Canadian shore of Lake Superior) these reservations are unpleasant social testimony to the changes forced upon the Chippewa by the coming of the white man. Once semi-nomadic forest-dwelling hunters, fishermen and wild-rice gathers, the Chippewa ranged over hundreds of thousands of square miles of northern Great Lakes forests. They lived in dome-shaped wigwams covered with birch bark and grass mats and were experts with the birchbark canoe. Today, theirs is a relatively sedentary way of life, either on or off the reservations. They are among the largest remnants of the aboriginal population in North America; approximately 80,000 live on reservation lands in the U. S. and Canada. An even larger number live off the reservations where they engage in a wide variety of occupations, among them agriculture, arts, education, law and medicine. A good place to visit the Chippewa people is at Assinins, the site of the Father Baraga mission, established in 1843 and now the Keweenaw Bay Tribal Center.

# Appendix F

## St. Germain

The town of St. Germain, located in the heart of the Wisconsin Northwoods, features a replica of the statue of Chief St. Germain, situated at the junction of Hwys. 70 and 155 near the information booth.

Indian names throughout the area can be attributed to the Chippewa, a tribe of the Algonquin stock. The word Chippewa is a lax attempt to say Ojibwa, which is usually translated to mean "to roast until puckered up" with reference to the wrinkled seams on the moccasins.

The Algonquins called the Wisconsin River "WeeKonsan," meaning "gathering of waters."

The name St. Germaine, spelled with an "e," dates back in records to the French soldier Jean Francois St. Germaine who married an Indian maiden and settled with his wife's tribe. He served with the armed forces as a guard for the fur traders until 1696 when the French government discontinued fur trading in the Northwoods.

Records are fragmentary. However, the name "St. Germain" has appeared many times in records as leaders among the Chippewa (Ojibwa) Indians. Beyond honoring these leaders, the statue of Chief St. Germain is meant to commemorate all Indians who used the area of St. Germain as one of their favorite hunting and fishing haunts and as their forested retreat, the name "St. Germain" meaning forest.

# Appendix G

## The Ojibwa Calendar

| | | |
|---|---|---|
| January | *Mulnedoo-Geezis* | Spirit Moon |
| February | *Nuhmabene-Geezis* | Sucker Moon |
| March | *Onahbune-Geezis* | The Moon of the Crust of the Snow |
| April | *Bobocquadahgiming-Geezis* | The Snow-shoe Breaking Moon |
| May | *Wahbegoone-Geezis* | The Moon of the Flowers |
| June | *Odaemene-Geezis* | The Strawberry Moon |
| July | *Misqueemene-Geezis* | The Raspberry Moon |
| August | *Meen-Geezis* | The Blueberry Moon |
| September | *Muhnoomene-Geezis* | The Wild Rose Moon |
| October | *Penahque-Geezis* | The Moon of the Falling Leaves |
| November | *Kushkudene-Geezis* | The Freezing Moon |
| December | *Muhnedoo-Geezisoons* | The Little Spirit Moon |

## An Ojibwa Glossary

| | |
|---|---|
| apples | *mish she min* |
| bad | *mon ah dis* |
| beans | *mis sqah dis a na nug* |
| bear | *mah quah* |
| birch bark | *we gwoss* |
| birchbark wigwam | *wigwass awigamig* |
| bread | *bah kwa ahi gun* |
| canoe | *ge mon* |

| | |
|---|---|
| cap | *we wah qwon* |
| chair | *ah pub ah win* |
| coat | *bis ah ka wa gun* |
| cold | *sin ah ma gud* |
| corn | *mun dah min* |
| cow | *bish i ka* |
| deer | *wah wah shkay she* |
| dog | *ah ne moosh* |
| eyes | *ga shkiah ig* |
| feet | *gis in dun* |
| floor | *mah chesug* |
| hand | *ah neen* |
| head | *shtig quhn* |
| hello | *bu shu* |
| house | *wan ki a gun* |
| Indian | *ah nih shnob ay* |
| meat | *we oss* |
| owl | *coo coo ah oo* |
| paleface | *che moh ka mon* |
| paper | *mus ih nich tig* |
| pepper | *ga we sah guow* |
| potatoes | *oh peh neeg* |
| salt | *ahi wah tah gun* |
| shoes | *muckisin* |
| soup | *ne boob* |
| sugar | *zen za baw gwad* |
| table | *duo poon* |
| water | *nih bih* |
| wigwam | *wigiwam* |

## Ojibwa Numerals

1 — *bay schig*
2 — *neeszh*
3 — *ni swee*
4 — *nee win*
5 — *nah nun*
6 — *een go dwah swee*
7 — *neeszh wah swee*

8 — *nish wah swi*
9 — *szhawng gah swee*
10 — *mee dah swee*
11 — *ah shee bay shig*
12 — *ah shee neesch*
13 — *ah shee nee swee*
14 — *ah shee nee win*
15 — *ah shee nah nun*
16 — *ah shee nong go dwah swee*
17 — *ah shee ne shwah see*
18 — *ah shee nish shwah swee*
19 — *ah shee shwang gah swee*
20 — *nee shtah nah*

# Appendix H
# Ojibwa Recipes

### Roast Wild Duck

Parboil duck with a small cleaned carrot, onion or garlic clove. Remove from water after one hour. Stuff bird with bread crumbs, salt, pepper, sage, onion, and roast until brown, basting in ½ hour, then add gravy when done. Currant jelly may be used to add spicy flavor. Serve.

### Potatoes Baked in Ashes

Wrap scrubbed potatoes in aluminum foil or wet bark or very wet leaves. Bury in hot ashes. Allow one hour for good-sized potatoes. Remove foil or leaves and serve with butter or margarine and salt.

### Roasted Corn on the Cob

Pull back husks and remove all silk. Replace husks and tie in place. Soak corn in salted water for 5 minutes, then drain. Roast on grill over hot fire for 10-12 min., turning frequently. Remove husks and serve corn with butter or margarine and salt. To roast in hot coals: After draining corn, bury in hot coals for 10-12 min.

### Roast Muskrat

Soak carcass in salt water overnight. Rinse in fresh

water. Place in baking dish with fresh water, salt, pepper, butter, and onions. (Spice and add herbs to taste.) Dredge and baste as it cooks, until done.

## Stewed Muskrat

Prepare same as Roast Muskrat. Cook in large kettle with additional water. Simmer until nearly done, then add in dozen small onions. Thicken sauce with flour and water mixture. Serve with sliced raw onions.

## Partridge with Sauerkraut

Ingredients:
2 partridges
2 thin slices of bacon
2 tablespoons butter
1¼ pounds of sauerkraut
1 chopped apple
1 tablespoon flour
salt and pepper

Season cleaned and dried birds with salt, pepper, and herbs to taste. Pin strip of bacon across each breast. Fry birds in butter for 15 minutes. Add sauerkraut. Add ¼ cup of water and apple. Cover and simmer for 2 hours. When birds are tender, remove from pan, then remove bacon strips. Add flour to sauerkraut and cook another 10 minutes.

## Fried Muskrat

Cut in quarters. Soak in salt water overnight. Rinse in fresh water, dry with clean cloth, and season to taste. Dip pieces in prepared egg batter, dust with flour, then brown quickly in a greased skillet. Then fry slowly for one hour.

## Barbecued Raccoon

Parboil carcass without seasoning until meat is tender but still firm. Rub with barbecue sauce. Place over barbecue pit or on a spit above fire. Baste with sauce (sage or garlic), brown and serve.

## Stewed Raccoon

Cut in small pieces and remove all fat. Boil in water until meat is tender but still firm. Add seasoning to taste. Skim off all fat. Thicken sauce with flour and water mixture.

## Wild Rice Stuffing

Add one teaspoon of salt to 3 quarts of boiling water. Add 2 cups of wild rice and boil until tender. Drain quickly. Steam if necessary until kernels separate. Saute 2 or 3 leaves celery and 1 minced onion in 3 tablespoons of butter. Add rice and saute 2 minutes, stirring frequently. Cool and stuff into bird.

## Roasted Wild Goose

Young geese may be roasted. Older ones have to be stewed. Prepare young geese the same as wild ducks. Skin older goose before cooking because the skin adds an unfavorable taste.

# INDEX

Author

# TOM HOLLATZ

# About the Author

Born and reared on the great South Side of Chicago, author Tom Hollatz was hooked on the fantastic sport of fishing at the age of five when his grandfather, who was also named Louis, took him out fishing day after day on Loon Lake near Antioch, Illinois. Later when the Northwoods of Wisconsin lured him to her crystal clear waters, Hollatz loved to hear the great fishing tales spun by the guides. His favorite fishing raconteur was the late guide Porter "Barefoot" Dean of Boulder Junction, Wisconsin.

Hollatz also owns a resort on Lake Minocqua and Cabin on the Lake in Boulder Junction, where he encourages young writers to write. He writes a monthly fishing column in several outdoor magazines.

Hollatz became sports editor of the Chicago *Daily Calumet* and later managing editor at the age of 25. His first day as an editor occurred on November 22, 1963, the day President Kennedy was assassinated. Later he moved to the Chicago *Tribune* where he stayed for 12½ years. At the *Tribune*, he was a copy editor and a photo editor. He was the night photo editor for four and a half years. He also wrote some travel articles and an occasional restaurant review.

He is currently doing what he loves to do most in the world — write. To paraphrase a popular power company slogan, Hollatz is a firm believer that the "Future belongs to the fishin'!"

Other books by Tom Hollatz are: *The White Earth Snowshoe Guide Book, The Guides of the Wisconsin Northwoods,* and *The Loon Book.*

970.3 Ho
Hollatz, Tom.
Louis no.1

## DATE DUE

| | | | |
|---|---|---|---|
| *apr.* | | | |
| *Aug* | | | |
| MY 28 96 | | | |
| | | | |
| | | | |
| | | | |
| | | | |
| | | | |
| | | | |
| | | | |
| | | | |
| | | | |